W9-BCF-477

In Christ

A SKETCH OF THE THEOLOGY OF ST. PAUL

In Christ

A SKETCH OF
THE THEOLOGY OF ST. PAUL

by Dr. William Grossouw
University of Nijmegen,
The Netherlands

*Translated and edited from the second revised Dutch
edition by* REV. MARTIN W. SCHOENBERG, O.S.C.

THE NEWMAN PRESS
WESTMINSTER, MARYLAND
1952

Originally published as
  In Christus, Schets van een Theologie van Sint Paulus
  by Uitgeverij Het Spectrum, Utrecht, Holland

Imprimi potest: Thomas A. Brandon, O.S.C.
            Vicar General

Nihil obstat: Aloysius J. Mehr, O.S.C.
          Censor Deputatus

Imprimatur: Louis B. Kucera
          Bishop of Lincoln

Library of Congress Catalog Card Number: 52–10389

Contents

Introduction

This little volume is written for Catholics—not for specialists in theology or Sacred Scripture. Consequently the author has tried to avoid as much as possible the use of technical terminology, which often proves a hindrance to the uninitiated and is for the initiated a convenient camouflage. Yet, since it was impossible to disregard technical terminology completely, he has tried to explain carefully such terms as could not be avoided.

In a sense it is utter foolishness to pretend to collect the main thoughts of St. Paul into a book of this size, or into any book for that matter. The author, too, is aware of this. Nevertheless, the consideration of two factors has urged him on in this bold attempt: the inestimable spiritual wealth of the

7

Pauline epistles, and the general ignorance of
Catholics as a whole of the very existence of these
great treasures. This latter fact is confirmed by the
scarcity of Dutch Catholic literature on the matter.[1]
There are only three worthwhile biographies of St.
Paul in our language. Outside of these, there is, as
far as I know, no literature from which the average
Catholic can really learn the ideas of St. Paul—a
situation which manifests such dire need and spiritual poverty that the writer seemed almost to hear
the echo of the words "For woe to me if I do not
preach the gospel."

It was this fact which encouraged him to put these
thoughts on paper, though he feels here more than
ever that he is but a beginner in speech, an *imperitus
sermone,* since the project of writing down the
thoughts of St. Paul has proved even more difficult
than anticipated. For they must be presented cor-
rectly, with their full meaning and without being
watered down or oversimplified. At the same time
they must remain intelligible to the average modern
reader.

[1] The same is even more true of such literature in our own
English language. The following books, however, are recommended
to the interested reader: McGarry: *Paul and the Crucified,* New
York, 1939; Bandas: *The Master-Idea of St. Paul's Epistles, or the
Redemption,* Bruges, 1925; Holzner: *Paul of Tarsus,* St. Louis,
1946; Prat: *The Theology of St. Paul,* Westminster, 1950.—Tr.

The attempt undertaken in these few pages is a gamble—an effort to give the reader some insight into the world of St. Paul's thoughts. Consequently there is no intention of narrating the story of his life and of his astounding apostolic activity. Nor shall we discuss the wonderful heritage he has left us in his epistles, or even explain any of them in particular. What we shall try to accomplish together (for your cooperation is indispensable) is to penetrate into his spiritual but very real world, to search out and follow the leading thoughts which animate and characterize his epistles and which have exercised an inestimable influence on Christianity. Hence our work will not be primarily biographical or historical or literary or even exegetic in the strict sense of the word, but theological.

Why is this a gamble? For many reasons. In the first place, modern man seems to harbor an aversion for writing of a theological tenor—and not without reason. Catholic theology, like any other science, is equipped with a terminology of its own, which authors seldom avoid successfully and which actually hinders the uninitiated. As far as the ordinary man is concerned this particular terminology soon becomes *Greek*. Add to this the fact that Paul himself —even abstracting from all the theological baggage which has been heaped upon him in the course of the centuries—is difficult, and uses language which was not easy to understand in his own time and was definitely not clear to everyone. He was an educated man, a professional in the Jewish theology of his time, possessing a ready knowledge of the Scriptures such as is hard to find in our day even in men of similar pursuits. And perhaps he supposes too readily, as is common among such people, that his readers can follow him and do actually understand his sharp insinuations and keen reasonings. Moreover, in his capacity of Apostle of the Gentiles, he was frequently involved in heated, even theoretical, disputes of a theological sort, disputes of which we find only the conclusions in his epistles. All these things make it difficult for us to understand his writings.

But we have not yet mentioned the chief reason, the one that really turns our efforts into a gamble, and yet at the same time urges us to take the risk: namely, that Paul *thinks* so profoundly. Difficult thoughts in a difficult language, that is what we are confronted with in his epistles. Yet we shall attempt at least to approach his ideas, for this—the search for the thoughts that are most properly his own— leads us to the real and imperishable Paul, insofar at least as it is possible to understand him and to establish a spiritual affinity with him. These thoughts are inspired by God and are thus perfectly "real," true to reality. They project our line of thought into the sphere of reality as it is known by God Himself; they bring it in contact with the very reality of God. For these thoughts, formulated with an incredible acumen by Paul, are the thoughts of God Himself, but expressed in the language of men. "Heaven and earth will pass away, but my words will not pass away." If our times have taught us anything at all, it is a sense of reality, a reality merciless and absolute, without air-castles or self-delusion. But there is one reality, as true as that of the senses and of the imagination, which the natural man (present in all of us) tends to pass by: the reality of sin and death, of redemption and grace, of expectation and resurrection, the reality of Christ and of God. It is this reality to which the Apostle introduces us. And we shall see that nothing is further away from him than a false idealism. He is a great realist.

The writer is convinced that our Catholic people (and he is not thinking only of the laity) do not know Paul. Even to the few who do know him, he is little more than a nodding acquaintance. What is more, these few do not make him their own—a truly personal spiritual possession, one which they can really understand and from which they can draw as from their own resources—in such a way that they

11

can give testimony and pray. This is truly a sad state of affairs!

The attentive reader must not suppose that these short chapters will give him the key to a full understanding of all the Pauline epistles. Only a few of the main ideas will be sketched here. He will note that even then almost every individual text will demand a detailed study. But the most basic foundation, at least, will perhaps have been laid.

We have fourteen letters of St. Paul, each differing in length and content. They are addressed to different persons or churches, and were written at quite different times. In the editions of the New Testament they are placed after the Acts of the Apostles in the following order: the Epistle to the Romans (Rom.), the First and the Second Epistles to the Corinthians (I and II Cor.), those to the Galatians (Gal.), the Ephesians (Eph.), the Philippians (Phil.), and to the Colossians (Col.), the First and the Second Epistles to the Thessalonians (I and II Thess.), the First and the Second Epistles to Timothy (I and II Tim.), and those to Titus (Tit.), to Philemon (Philem.), and to the Hebrews (Hebr.). All of them are in fact occasional letters, as are most letters at any time. They were brought about by special circumstances and have a special purpose. Hence they are not theological treatises or essays.

Yet the greater number of them are not of such a personal and intimate character as are ours, because St. Paul's letters generally treat of matters which are of common interest and are addressed to local churches or persons in authority. The short letter to Philemon is an exception; it is of a special kind, which has its own place even among letters of antiquity. The epistles were dictated, as was customary at that time. Sometimes Paul would add a concluding note in his own hand. By no means are they the products of an office. They have their origin in real life. Because they have been occasioned by special questions or circumstances we may not expect in them a calm, well-weighed, and completely detailed treatment of a theological sort. When Paul speaks about marriage in I Cor. 7, it is because of determined circumstances—the situation of *newly* converted Christians in frivolous Corinth. The letter is meant for them. Hence we must not be surprised if we do not find in it a detailed exposition of the meaning of Christian marriage adapted to all times and places. However, the fact that we do find such a thorough exposition in these letters is due to the enlightened faith and noble spirit of the Apostle, who knows how to elevate even the ordinary daily questions to a high and lasting level.

The more important among the epistles are the

13

four commonly known as the major epistles; namely, the one to the Romans, the two to the Corinthians and the one to the Galatians. Next in rank are the so-called Captivity Epistles—those to the Ephesians, the Colossians, and the Philippians. We will not pay any special attention to the Epistle to the Hebrews, which has a character all its own. The most profound (and the most difficult) of them all is the one to the Romans. But it is also the closest approach toward a systematic treatise—at least in the first part.

These are the sources from which we hope to draw our material. Leaving aside all details—even some very important ones, because there are so many —we will attempt to point out only the leading thoughts and the chief principles. We will have to arrange whatever remains. To enable ourselves to understand the Apostle it is desirable that we seek an order which is consonant with his line of thinking, not one borrowed from our own. The logical as well as the historical point of departure for his theological process of thought is the condition of unredeemed man.

CHAPTER ONE

Existence Without Christ

THE STARTING POINT OF PAUL'S thought is not merely this or that idea about human nature, but the whole man as he is in reality, as he is seen by God. It is the reality of unredeemed man, man without Christ. Paul sees this state as an existence under the influence of sin, *an existence in the flesh, an existence condemned to death.* Without Christ man is hopelessly doomed. Sin rules as a tyrant; the flesh renders him incapable of resistance; death is inevitable. This is his lot. "All have sinned and have need of the glory of God" (Rom. 3:23). No individual man, nor all men together, can free him from this state. Life and justification are beyond his reach. Thus the factors which make up human existence in its unredeemed state are sin, the flesh, and death. For the Jew, the Law must be added.

I. *Sin*

In the first place there is the notion—or rather the reality—of *sin*. Here already we come upon the parting of many ways. Paul's teaching is one of redemption, just as Christianity is essentially a religion of redemption. Hence the idea of redemption is very important for an understanding of his whole teaching. Christianity does not redeem from matter, but from sin. Paul says this expressly: "redemption, [which is] the remission of sins" (Eph. 1:7; Col. 1:14). Thus the notion of *sin* is of the utmost importance in order to understand him. For if Christianity includes redemption from sin, then sin is the ruling factor in a life that is not Christian. And this is precisely what St. Paul says.

Where the notion of sin is lost, as it is to a great extent in the modern world, Christianity may be compared to a clanging bell in a deserted village. We may only hope that the effects of sin—fear, misery, and death—which have afflicted our generation so grievously, will again open the eyes of mankind to the reality underlying them.

16

To Paul sin is not just a juridical notion of an infinite offense against the divine majesty. It is disobedience to God's will and law; it is open revolt against God, causing a state of enmity with God, which leads to death. Sinful man is estranged from God. He is the object of God's wrath which will break upon him on the day of judgment. He is a child of death. The most pertinent texts concerning this matter are to be found in the first part of the letter to the Romans, especially in chapters 5–8. Even as a matter of pure statistics, the words which express sin or related ideas occur more frequently here than in any other part of the whole New Testament. When Paul looks at the sinfulness of man his realistic pessimism is very evident. It is not his intention, as is so often the case among us, to excuse or to ignore this reality with a sort of collective complacency. If there is one thing which he expresses without ambiguity or hesitation it is the prevalence of sin in the non-Christian man, whether Jew or pagan. "All have sinned and have need of the glory of God" (Rom. 3:23). "But the Scripture shut up all things under sin" (Gal. 3:22). He proves this point by an appeal to experience and to Scripture, hence by an appeal to divine revelation and to facts, and not by the use of fanciful theories. He does this in a manner both perplexing and disarming in Romans 1–3 and

17

applies it to the Jews as well as to the pagans. In his view, all mankind was divided into two categories, as far as the religious aspect was concerned: the small minority, which had received the Law of God through revelation; and the large, undefined multitude, which had the law of God written in their hearts, but carried it with them as in a daze or in a drunken stupor. Still for them their conscience was always a law.

But both categories are equally and hopelessly lost without Christ, for both—that is, all men—have sinned. In Romans 1:18–32 Paul begins a pointed accusation against both heathen idolatry and heathen immorality. The Jew listens with inner consent. It has long been his conviction that the pagans are sinners and "impure." Suddenly Paul turns to him and says: "Wherefore thou art inexcusable, O man, whoever thou art who judgest. For wherein thou judgest another, thou dost condemn thyself" (Rom. 2:1). All your religious privileges of which you are so proud—circumcision, the Law, and all the words of God—all of them gain you nothing because you are in fact sinning as much as the Greek and the barbarian. And he closes this passage with an unforgettable array of quotations from the Scriptures, arranged in a special manner against the Jew, for he also must believe in the sinfulness of all men, "in order that every mouth may be shut, and the whole world may be made subject to God " (Rom. 3:19).

Paul does not stop here. He is not satisfied with asserting that sin is universal because all partake of it by sinful deeds. He looks upon sin as a power outside and above the individual man. It is a despot tyrannizing the world. The tyrant *Sin, Hamartia,* took its hold upon mankind with Adam's fall (Rom. 5:12). It exercises regal power, which in antiquity meant absolute power (Rom. 5:21). Sin is an absolute master whose servants we are, and death is its reward to those who serve it—in other words, to all (Rom. 6:16, 23). It was powerless before the institution of the Law, but with the *Torah* [1] it got new life and new strength wherewith to work evil and to beguile and kill man (Rom. 7:7 ff.). Only Christ's death has uprooted sin in its very foundation (Rom. 8:3).

Paul speaks of sin as a person. Of course this is not carried to such an extent that we are to look at it in a mythological manner, as though evil were some sort of malignant spirit. It is rather a figure of speech, but one that has its justification in the shocking reality which it is meant to suggest—namely, the universal and compelling power, one might al-

---

[1] Torah: the Jewish Law, as contained in the Pentateuch, the first five books of the Old Testament.

most say the irresistible destiny, of sin. *Almost,* because Paul never loses sight of the freedom of the will (no right-thinking Jew would even dream of doing so). But without worrying too much about the logical connection between freedom and universal sinfulness, he is utterly aware of that reality, from which we are only too ready to withdraw our attention, namely, the tyranny of sin over mankind. He views the multiplicity and variety of sinful actions as a domineering superhuman power. Sin is, for Paul, a merciless slave driver, which avails itself of the flesh and the Law and has as its consequence eternal death. "Now the sting of sin is death, and the power of sin is the Law" (I Cor. 15:56). At the same time this personification of sin as a being outside of man indicates a certain pity for man himself. Paul regards sin not only as a conscious act of revolt against God, but also as the "fate" of unredeemed man; as a tyrant who has the stumbling children of Adam under his thumb, from whose control they cannot wrest themselves without Christ. He does not disregard their responsibility; yet sin is stronger than the individual man. This is the full reality which underlies those crude images. It is also the teaching of the Church that man by himself is not always capable of doing what is good.[2]

[2] For example, see Denziger, 793.

20

II. *The Flesh*

Whence does sin acquire this compelling power over mankind? According to Paul's teaching it is principally from two sources: the flesh and the Law.

Flesh is a term which we are no longer accustomed to use in this special connotation. Among the Jews it customarily meant the (living) body—the body as the weaker and the transitory part of man. Because of this the whole man and mankind itself could be looked upon as trifling, a powerless thing when compared to God. This is the import of the words: "Blessed art thou, Simon Bar-Jona, for flesh and blood has not revealed this to thee, but my Father in heaven." This was the customary usage; it is always the Biblical one. Paul continues this line of thought especially in the *moral* order. He sees a close relation between sin and the flesh. This is the way he looks at it. The flesh—which is to say: the body, the human part—weakens a man in regard to the moral good which his reason or the Law prescribes. This weakness is the result of the passions and the desires of the flesh, which become activated in and express themselves through the members of the body. These desires are opposed to those of the spirit. They lead a man to evil and thus to death (Gal. 5:16–17, 24; Rom. 6:19; 8:6–7; 13:14, etc.). Do not suppose that Paul considers sexual sins as the worst ones. He is indeed realistic enough to acknowledge the great havoc wrought upon mankind by sexual immorality. He considers the disgraceful unnatural impurity of many pagans of his day as a punishment which God inflicted upon them because of something much more basic—their refusal to give God the honor due Him (Rom. 1). Among the deeds of the flesh enumerated in Galatians 5 and in Romans 13 there are also many other sins which have a more immaterial character, such as offenses against charity and justice.

The flesh—the corporal part of man, man himself as he exists in actuality—is the source of self-interest. It instills in him many desires. It leads him to countless sinful deeds.

Yet, according to Paul, the relation between the body of death and sin is still closer. It is not without reason that he speaks of "sinful flesh" (Rom. 8:3) and the "body of sin" (Rom. 6:6). In his opinion the flesh is the port of entry, the headquarters, and the tool of sin (especially in Rom. 7). Speaking in the name of the unredeemed, he says: "I am carnal, sold into the power of sin" (Rom. 7:14). *Because* I am *carnal* (*sarkinos*), I am expropriated and subject to the power of sin. Through the flesh, which is a part of myself and at the same time contrives as a fifth column with the enemy outside, sin has civil rights and free entry. Through the

flesh sin is active within me; the flesh is its instrument. It continually places its desires and members
at the service of sin.

Just as Paul does not deny the freedom of the
will, so he does not identify sin and the flesh (see,
for example, Rom. 6:12–19; 8:3; 12:1; II Cor. 4:
11). But in his realistic pessimism he again under-
lines the close affinity which actually does exist between sin and the body. Indeed he does not idealize
at all.

In consequence of his factual composition (that
is, because of the element called "flesh"), man is
abandoned to sin as long as he has not received the
spirit of Christ. This is the psychological explanation
of the universality of sin. Is the corporal in man
such *by its very nature?* Paul does not say that. He
says that *in fact* it is so. He is satisfied to say only
that—yet how dramatic, and how impressive! Only
once does he indicate that the flesh has *become* what
it is, that the inclination to evil, as it is usually
called, is a consequence of original sin;[3] because he
says explicitly that as a result of Adam's sin all men
are subjected to the power of sin (Rom. 5:12, 19).
When thus two chapters later in the same Epistle he

---

[3] The inclination toward evil, the egoism of man, is not itself
sinful, but it is a propensity which leads to sin (to sinful acts of
the will) and is so forcible in fallen man that, taken as a whole,
it cannot be overcome without grace.

23

explains the universal power of sin because of man's carnal constitution, we are compelled to combine the psychological and historical explanation and to conclude that the relationship between sin and the flesh is not indeed a natural one, as we say, but one which had its historical origin in the first sin of man. Nevertheless, this "historical" origin is so close to the very origin of the human race that Paul, speaking of the Jews, can rightly say: "We were *by nature* children of wrath [of God] even as the rest" (Eph. 2:3).

III. *The Law*

Now for the *Law,* the external factor which, according to Paul, has cooperated most with the flesh, the internal factor in man, in bringing man into the clutches of sin. This constitutes a point on which the average Catholic generally makes two observations. First: How difficult to understand! Secondly (when with great pains he has grasped the matter to some extent): What good does it do me? Does it still have any use for us? Such remarks cannot be sidestepped; we must try to answer them. Opposition to the Judaism of his day plays an important role both in Paul's life and in his letters. It is a thing hard to understand and still harder to evaluate properly. Here too we discover the real Paul—in the polemic with the so-called Judaizers; that is to say, with those Jews who had become Christians, but who wished to bring their whole Jewish past with them into the Church and attached more value to their old Law than to the redemption of Christ. As in every polemic, so here we miss a host of details with the ramifications they had at that time but which were later lost. Yet Paul deals even with actual problems in such a profound manner and from such an exalted plane that here, too, he strikes on eternal truths, on ever-recurring bents of soul. To put it more directly: the Law about which he speaks is the Jewish Law, the Mosaic Torah. It is this Law which his adversaries wished to impose as the only means of salvation even upon Paul's Christians, and *in the same sense* in which they themselves practiced it. This the Apostle opposed with all his might. He fought the battle and won it. Even at the time of the Gospel of St. John, a generation later, Judaism in the Church was a thing of the past. The dispute actually centered upon a question of a temporal and passing nature, though it was a vital one and of the greatest importance. It was a stage of development in the growth of the young Church. But Paul handles the situation in such a masterful manner that he has typified and silenced the servile

man. For the servile man is a character of all times
—a man who wittingly or unwittingly seeks his salvation only in the external observance of all precepts. Even today there are Christians who forget
that we are saved by God's grace and by faith in
Jesus, together with the works of love which are
subsequent to it but emanate from it, or, as Paul
prefers to say, "the fruit of the Spirit" (Gal. 5:22).

How does the Law become a factor in the fatal
plot which we have just seen sin and death contrive
against unredeemed man? But for a few and clearly
indicated exceptions, Paul always uses the word Law
for the Torah, the Law of Moses, the content of the
Pentateuch (the first five books of the Old Testament). This Torah is a huge complex of various
precepts—moral, ritual, juridical and social—which
regulated the entire Jewish life. In it are contained,
for example, the ten commandments, the prohibi-
tion of swine's flesh, the Israelitic law on slavery, as
well as the penal law. In the course of time these
laws were multiplied by numerous interpretations,
the so-called "traditions of the elders," whose purpose was to determine the Torah for all possible
occasions which were not foreseen by the Law of
Moses. According to the Pharisees these interpretations carried the same obligation as the Torah itself.
It required a complete study to know all of them.

The average Jew was not capable of this, and yet everyone who was circumcised was obliged to observe the whole Law. This principle is also accepted by Paul (Gal. 5:3).

Paul considers the Torah *en bloc* as the Law of God, as the revelation of God's will in the Old Covenant; and as such it is "good, just, holy, even spiritual" (Rom. 7:12, 14). It is the great religious prerogative of the Jews (Rom. 3:1; 9:4). And yet, the Law is the great accomplice of sin! Here we hit upon a startling example of what was termed above the fidelity of Paul's thought to reality (and thus also its complexity, because reality is not simple). Here we detect the actually multiple import of the Torah. Let us consider it under its various aspects and then try to view them as a whole in the unity of God's plan.

The Law, the expression of God's will, is in itself holy and good. Though calculated to arouse the approbation of man's rational insight (Rom. 7:16, 22), it is nonetheless incapable of effecting his salvation. For the Law is but "the letter," that is to say, a command put down in writing, but still something outside of man himself—something which leaves him just as he was: carnal. It presents itself to man's consciousness as certain definite, divine ordinances, but does not give him the power to com-

27

ply with them. It is a dead letter, even a *deadening* one, for it brings capital punishment upon all offenders. Thus we are faced with the opposition between the letter of the Old Covenant, and the spirit, the internal life-giving principle of Christianity (Rom. 2:27; 7:6; II Cor. 3:6–7). This essential impotence of each law as such for effecting God's demands becomes, in unredeemed man, the stark reality of sin. The reason for this is the *flesh,* which is inclined *toward* sin and *against* the Law. The Law actually accents the situation in favor of sin, and that in spite of itself, because it gives the knowledge of sin *but no more* (Rom. 3:20; 7:7). The effect is that what would otherwise have remained a semi-consciously sinful act, an inattention to a vague and indefinite voice of the natural law, becomes a formal violation of the will of God recognized as such. Through the Law sin becomes a *transgression* (*parabasis*), a positive breach of the divine will clearly known. Through the Law's many precepts the number of consciously sinful deeds is unspeakably increased. For the Torah removes the natural unconcern of the pagan. Through the Law sin is able to manifest its infernal, God-hating aspect (Rom. 7:13).

Is this view of sin unfair or one-sided? Keep in mind that the starting point of Paul's polemic was the Pharisaic Jewry of his own time and his personal past. Pharisaic Jewry considered the observances of the Law, the "works of the Law," as the only source of salvation: "A man is justified by the works of the Law." These works were, *in their view,* undertaken by one's self and accomplished by one's own power, without the grace of God and the hope of the Messias.[4] Through this self-justification even the Law becomes pernicious as a source of lies and self-deification (Rom. 3:27; Phil. 3:9; Rom. 10:3).

What then is the purpose of the Law? This is the question Paul and we ask next (Gal. 3:19–22; Rom. 5:20). Since the Law comes from Him, what part can it possibly have had in God's plan of salvation? Was it not a great failure? Paul's judgment in the matter, his Christian judgment about the Law, formulated in the light of Christ's death, is that the Torah has a proper positive role, though a subordinate one. He expresses this role by the startling words: "Now the Law intervened that the offense might abound" (Rom. 5:20).[5] "It was enacted on ac-

---

[4] The necessity of grace was not denied by Pharisaism in *theory,* but their concept of religion led to a negation of its necessity in *practice.*

[5] This is the way the Confraternity of Christian Doctrine edition of the New Testament translates the verse. The Greek original, however, seems to be a bit more forceful. It uses a compound verb, *pareiserchomai,* with not only one, but two prepositions, *para-eis-erchomai.* The meaning is that the Law was added

29

count of transgressions" (Gal. 3:19). What does this mean? It means that God foresaw that the Law would be the occasion of many sins. He permitted this and used this possibility of the defection of man's free will as a useful element in His economy of salvation. The Law activated sin, which was already present in the world as a great power, and rendered it extremely productive of transgressions. God permitted this in order that the light of grace and redemption might appear all the brighter against so dark a background (Rom. 5:20–21). He permitted sin to gain the mastery even of the Jews, His chosen people, so that *all* were thus subject to sin and had to appear powerless before God and thus give glory to God alone when they were redeemed. Salvation had to be pure grace and mercy so that no man might boast in God's presence (Rom. 3:19–20; 7:13; 11:32; Gal. 3:22). In Paul's line of thought the idea that the Law intensified the consciousness of universal sinfulness and thus increased the desire for redemption is only secondary. He rather looked at the objective order of God's plan, in which the Law, having its origin in God, becomes partner of God's adversary, sin, and nevertheless ultimately serves God's purpose. God's glory alone: this is

---

over and above sin. Cf. Zorell, *Lexikon Graecum Novi Testamenti,* Paris, 1931.—Tr.

Paul's deepest and most fruitful thought. The Law itself also manifests God's glory because it exposes the foolishness of all human self-glorification in a very clear, though paradoxical, manner. Whatever comes from God and whatever man with his reason recognizes as coming from God (Rom. 7:14, 22) only produces sin in our body of death, as long as God has not overcome sin in the flesh of Jesus Christ (Rom. 8:3).

IV. *Death*

Thus sin finds nourishment on all sides, in the flesh of man and in the Law of God. It grows and increases in strength. Sin begets sin through scandal taken from others and through the even more oppressive slavery of bad habits in the sinner himself (Rom. 6:19, 23). It thus becomes the normal condition, the ordinary state of man. It continually estranges him from God, whose enemy he becomes (Rom. 5:8–10; Col. 1:21, etc.). God's wrath rests upon him as a dead weight, which will some day crush him and will reveal itself for what it really is on the day of universal judgment (Rom. 1:18). Thus sin brings forth its only, though bitter, fruit— *death*. "As through one man sin entered into the world and through sin death, thus death has passed into all men because all have sinned" (Rom. 5:12).

31

Death, the great enemy at large, enters immediately through the breach which sin has broken into the wall of mankind. In Paul's view, death is not a natural, and consequently an indifferent, phenomenon. It is the punishment for sin, to which all are subject because all have become sinners in Adam. Through Christ's death it loses its sting, which is sin (I Cor. 15:55–57). Only at the parousia [6] and the resurrection will this last enemy be utterly vanquished (I Cor. 15:26).

It is only when we have in some degree obtained an over-all view of Paul's ideas on unredeemed man that we are enabled to understand and experience the full force of such a sentence as Rom. 7:5, in which—speaking of his own experience too—he summarizes the state of man's existence without Christ: "For when we were in the *flesh,* the *sinful passions,* which were aroused by the *Law,* were at work in our *members* so that they brought forth fruit unto *death.*" Such is man without Christ: a slave of sin, subject to the Law, living in the flesh, doomed to death. His is a life which of itself leads to death, and thus should not even be called life.

Paul sees the power of sin extended over even irrational creatures, because they suffer in conjunction with man, who ought to be their king: "For

[6] Parousia: the second coming of Christ at the end of time.

32

creation was made subject to vanity . . . to the slavery of corruption. . . . For we know that all creation groans and travails in pain until now" (Rom. 8:19–22).

To complete this sombre and distressing picture we must add the absolute impotence of man, whether Jew or Gentile, to free himself from this situation: "For we have argued that Jews and Greeks are all under sin, as it is written: There is not one just man, not even one" (Rom. 3:9–10).[7] "For those who rely on the works of the Law are under a curse" (Gal. 3:10).

Shall we rise here and just forget about the whole matter? Shall we step out into the fresh breeze of the evening and shake off the sombre picture? Shall we say that it no longer applies to our times? Or should we rather acknowledge that, looking from the plenitude of Christ, Paul views the spiritual *situation* as it really is, and that it is only our lack of faith and our superficial attitude which hinder us from sharing the deep compassion with which the Apostle sketches the tragic picture of the pagan of all times: "having no hope, and without God in the world" (Eph. 2:12)?

[7] This is the reading of the original Greek. The Confraternity edition has, "There is not one just man; there is none who understands . . ."

CHAPTER TWO

Redemption in Christ

*I*N THE PREVIOUS CHAPTER WE delved with Paul into the depth of human misery. Man, as man, is doomed and incapable of helping himself. No matter how impressive his accomplishments may be in the field of science or art, of technique or of the mastery of natural forces, he remains hopelessly deficient in the essential human values of morality and religion. Sin is not an accidental bagatelle of human life, not even a merely regrettable incident, but a power which has established mastery over man. It has imbedded itself in his flesh, and there it has become fertile and active. It becomes a

35

condition which determines and rules his entire existence: enmity with God, the wrath of God, death, and exclusion from eternal life. The God-given Law serves only to aggravate the situation. Through its impotence on the one hand, and the consciousness of sin which it arouses on the other, it brings to a climax the crisis of irredemption.

In this state, sin is the factor which determines and rules everything. No wonder that Nietzsche, in *Die fröhliche Wissenschaft* (Aph. 135) and elsewhere, directs his darts against what he terms the fiction of lese majesty against divinity. But he forgets that while sin does not actually touch the divine essence, it is a horrible reality in man. It is loss of life, just as Paul tells us. No wonder that in their great work *Soviet Communism: A New Civilization,* the Webbs state that the foundation of official ethics in Russia consists in removing the idea of sin (page 839).

What Paul formulated so precisely in the light of revelation and with the help of divine inspiration is no more than what has been felt by the consciousness of all ages, and what even the pagan cults attempted to express in their numberless expiatory rites. Man occupies a position of indebtedness toward the Divinity. He has a responsibility toward it. But he lacks the ability to pay off the debt and to appease the wrath of God. "All have sinned and have need of the glory of God."

Against the background of this dark reality and in the midst of this absolute helplessness, the Apostle sees the great beneficence of God, redemption in Christ. What no man could do, "what was impossible to the Law, in that it was weak because of the flesh, God has made good. By sending his Son in the likeness of sinful flesh as a sin-offering, he has condemned sin in the flesh" (Rom. 8:3).

This will be the subject matter of the following pages. It is frequently called "objective redemption." Paul calls it "redemption in Christ." But first, a word concerning terminology. It is well to distinguish between objective and subjective redemption. The first is the redemptive death and resurrection of Christ. The second is the sanctification of the individual man, insofar as he is incorporated into Christ through faith and baptism. By the first, mankind is somehow or other redeemed in principle. By the second, the individual man is factually and concretely redeemed, freed from sin and sanctified. In our times we often speak of the meriting of grace through Christ's death (objective redemption) and the application of these merits to man (subjective redemption). This manner of representation has its merits, but it does not completely convey Paul's view of the redemption. Others prefer a terminology different from objective and subjective redemption; but all distinguish between what happened *in* and *through Christ,* and what happens *within man* (through Christ). This distinction helps make matters clearer and has a definite theological advantage. It is likewise in complete harmony with the teaching of the Apostle, though Paul does not always insist on it. The reasons for this will become clear later on. It will also become clear that at times a gain in clarity and in the analysis of an idea brings with it a loss of life and vigor.

I. *The Incarnation*

In Paul's theology, then, this is the place of Christ, of His incarnation, of His death and His resurrection from the dead. In the eyes of the Apostle it is the pivotal point of all history. For Paul, Jesus is the Head of the Church, the Lord of all, the perfect Image of the invisible God, the Son of God, God Himself. How precious Jesus has become to the persecutor of the early Church! How He has become the very center of his whole being! Many texts testify to this love with burning words, and are the first expression of love for the man Christ Jesus known to Christianity. "For me to live is Christ. . . . [I] desire to depart and to be with Christ, a lot by far the better. . . ." (Phil. 1:21, 23). "With Christ I am nailed to the cross. It is now no longer I that live, but Christ lives in me. And the life that I now live in the flesh, I live in the faith of the Son of God, who loved me and gave himself up for me" (Gal. 2:19–20).

Regardless of how much he is enamored of the love of Christ, regardless of how much he is convinced that our salvation rests in Him alone, Paul looks even higher for the source of redemption. His idea of God is his most operative one. God is the source of all initiative. To Him alone all honor is due. This is particularly true of the redemption (Rom. 3:25; II Cor. 5:18–19, etc.). The source of all salvation (thus, of the redemption in Christ) is God's merciful *decree.* This is the great *mystery,* the great secret of God, which fills Paul and concerning which he almost waxes poetic in his Epistle to the Ephesians.[1]

Paul calls this decree of God to redeem man— earthy man—through the man Christ, a *mystery.*[2] This mystery was hidden in the bosom of the Divinity. It was indeed foreshadowed in the Mes-

---

[1] Cf. Eph. 1:3, 9–10, etc.; Rom. 16:25–27; I Cor. 2:7, etc.

[2] Mystery: a secret. In Paul's usage it means God's eternal decree to save the world in and through Christ and His Church. This decree was originally hidden, but has been made known by the apostolic preaching of the gospel.

sianic promises of the Old Testament. But these texts were obscure, their interrelation was not clear and outstanding; and hence they could be fully understood only in the light of their fulfillment. Indeed the fulfillment of these promises, the beginning of their actualization, through Christ's death and resurrection and through the Church, His body, has disclosed the mystery. And the news of this revelation is now given to the world through the gospel— the joyful news of the fulfillment. It is made known through the apostolic preaching—God's invitation to man to the homage of faith. The mystery is not secretive; the veils of the Old Testament have been cast aside. Boldly and proudly, as Paul says, we preach to all, to Jew and to Gentile. Yet it remains a mystery, for only faith penetrates into the meaning of the facts. To the powers of the world and to their followers, the cross of Jesus remains only a cross—simultaneously a scandal and utter folly. The reason for God's saving decree is exclusively His mercy (Rom. 15:8–9; 11:32), His grace (5:15; Eph. 1:6–7, etc.), His sovereign free love (Rom. 5:8). It is literally unfathomable, with no explanation but the abyss of God's infinite being. How could it be otherwise? All have sinned and all are enemies of God. For this reason, it would almost seem that Paul takes pleasure in describing man's misery and impotence, in order that the honor of God, the glory of His merciful grace, may be exalted thereby. There was *nothing* outside of God which could move Him to interfere and to save man. Hence also the actualization of this decree, the factual redemption of man, shall rise wholly as praise to the throne of God. The ultimate end of it all is *in laudem gloriae gratiae,* the glorious praise of His sheer mercy (Eph. 1:6, etc.). And this decree existed from all *eternity*. "For those whom he has foreknown he has also predestined to become conformed to the image of his Son that he should be the firstborn among many brethren" (Rom. 8:29). From all eternity God foresaw the sin of Adam and the sins of mankind, and from all eternity He had decreed man's redemption through Jesus Christ. When we ask ourselves why God permitted sin with all its dreadful results, we must always remember that we are faced with the mystery of human freedom and dignity, and, therefore, with the mystery of man's relationship toward his Creator. God created man because of love, to have him participate in His own goodness and happiness. He created him in His own image and likeness and endowed him with the royal gift of freedom which elevates him above matter. It is precisely because of this that man, who is neither God nor eternally confirmed in God, can fall away from God, can sin. In man's freedom is contained the supreme possibility for good or evil. That is why it is his glory, and can be his ruin. God asks for a free love which honors Him infinitely more than the necessary love of irrational creatures. This free love alone makes us happy. Paul adds that what sin has destroyed is abundantly restored in Christ (Rom. 5: 15–21). The means which Christ gave us for overcoming sin and its effects *in us* will be considered later.

What is contained in this divine plan, which is sheer mercy and had been determined from all eternity? What is the content of that *mystery?* How had God determined from all eternity to redeem man? *Through and in Christ:* through His death and resurrection (the objective redemption) and through the incorporation of the individual man into Himself (the subjective redemption through faith and baptism, through the Church and final perseverance), "this grace has abounded beyond measure in us in all wisdom and prudence, so that he may make known to us the mystery of his will according to his good pleasure. And this his good pleasure he purposed in him to be dispensed in the fulness of the times; to re-establish all things in Christ, both those in the heavens and those on the earth" (Eph. 1:9–10). Thus the mystery has two aspects, which really

42

may not be separated: the redemptive works of the personal Christ, His death and resurrection, and the working of grace in the mystical Christ, the Church. In this chapter we shall speak of the first aspect—of Jesus' death and resurrection as the basis of our redemption.

Paul's terminology is entirely directed to his soteriology.[3] To put it more simply: in the eyes of the Apostle, Christ is always the Redeemer. He is aware of the three phases of His existence: His so-called preexistence as Son of God in the divine nature which is properly His (Phil. 2:7), His life in mortal flesh, and His glorious existence as Son of God in power after the resurrection. This last is the view which Paul prefers to take of Him—the glori-fied Lord as He appeared to Paul at Damascus and called him from his state of *non-existence* to the glory and honor of the apostolate, to be the last chosen, but an authentic witness of the resurrection.

For Paul, Jesus is undoubtedly God, even in His capacity for suffering. We will not discuss that point now. It is evident from the assurance with which he simply calls Him the Son of God. But whenever he speaks of Jesus as Redeemer, he considers Him in His human nature whether suffering or glorious. This must be noted once and for all.

[3] Christology: the theological doctrine on the person of Christ. Soteriology: the theological doctrine on the redemption.

43

II. *Christ's Death on the Cross*

In what exactly does God's secret of redemption consist? In this: that He willed to send His Son in the unredeemed state of fallen man. God willed this insofar as was *metaphysically* possible (and that appeared to be quite far, much further than any man had dared to suppose). God redeemed man not merely from afar, as a distant but benevolent stranger, but in a most intimate fashion.

The factors which constitute and determine the unredeemed state of man have become, as it were, essential elements of Jesus' own existence. Christ, the only Son of God's love, has "emptied" Himself (Phil. 2:7). He freely relinquished the divine prerogatives which were His. He actually assumed our human existence. He suffered it, and so conquered our state of irredemption in His own person. This person does not exist for its own sake but, as *Head* of the new humanity, has become through death and resurrection the source and exemplar of redeemed human existence. The glorified Lord who is present before God's throne and also upon our altars is no ideal, paradisiacal man, but the Lamb which was immolated and which forever bears the marks of Its wounds before the throne of the Father. "For our sakes he made him to be *sin* who knew nothing of

44

sin" (II Cor. 5:21). "By sending his Son in the likeness of sinful flesh as a sin-offering, he has condemned sin in the flesh [of Christ] (Rom. 8:3)," "in his body of flesh" (Col. 1:22, etc.). "God sent his Son, born of a woman, born under the Law" (Gal. 4:4; 3:13). Christ took the nature of a slave and humbled Himself by becoming obedient to *death,* even to death on the cross (Phil. 2:7–8, etc.). Thus all the elements—sin, flesh, the law and death —which enslaved man were taken up by Christ and were overcome by Him. And we, too, overcame their tyranny because we all had part in Him.

It is impossible, and not at all necessary, to summarize here all the texts in which Paul speaks about the redemptive power of Christ's *death.* He constantly returns to this point. Christ took the curse of the Law upon Himself. The Law exercised its full power in Him and upon Him. It killed Him, and by doing so exhausted itself and brought about its own end in His death (Gal. 3:10 ff.). He has borne the punishment due to us for our sin (Rom. 8:32; 4:25, etc.). His death paid the penalty for our misdemeanors. We have been purchased by His blood (Col. 1:14; I Cor. 6:20; 7:32; Rom. 3:24, etc.). Through His death we have been "re-deemed," freed from sin. Thus we belong to Him, not to ourselves. Jesus' death has appeased the wrath of the

Father (Rom. 3:25). He was an offering acceptable to God (Gal. 2:20; Eph. 5:2, 26; I Cor. 11:25), the greatest proof of God's love for man, who was a sinner and His enemy (Rom. 5:8).

Let us read one text in its entirety (II Cor. 5:14–21): "For the love of Christ impels us, because we have come to the conclusion that, since one died for all, therefore all died; and that Christ died for all, in order that they who are alive may live no longer for themselves, but for him who died for them and rose again. . . . But all things are from God, who has reconciled us to himself through Christ and has given to us the ministry of reconciliation. For God was truly in Christ, reconciling the world to himself by not reckoning against men their sins and by entrusting to us the message of reconciliation. . . . For our sakes he made him to be sin who knew nothing of sin, so that in him we might become the justice of God."

In this passage are contained all the characteristics of Paul's teaching on the redemption. It is God who reconciled the world to Himself in and through Christ. God made Him to be sin for our sakes. Because of Him God no longer takes account of our sins—God, the first and the last, the efficient causality of all things. What is more, God redeems us *in* Christ. We prefer to say: *through* Christ. Both expressions are true and do not exclude each other; yet Paul prefers the first, because his teaching on the redemption is dominated by the great principle of *solidarity*. The man Christ who willed to share in our existence represents us all. He is the new Adam, the Head of reborn humanity, who includes all in Himself (Rom. 5:14; I Cor. 15:20–22, 45; Col. 1: 18; II Cor. 5:14). For Paul this is absolute reality. It is so self-evident that in his letters he speaks of it only in passing. "One has died for all, thus all have died," he shouts. When Jesus died on the cross, all of us died with Him, and in Him. When on Calvary He laid down His "body of flesh," He overcame death and exhausted the Law, and through His death annulled it. At the same time all of us, at least in principle, overcame the factors which constitute our state of irredemption. Now there is only question of the individual man entering through faith and baptism into the community which is "in Christ" and so becoming partaker of His glorious life. For this reason, too, His death has vicarious worth. He suffered the death which we deserved for our sins.

III. *The Resurrection*

Though it is short, this must suffice to give us some insight into the significance of Christ's death

47

on the cross according to the teaching of Paul. This point will be taken up again when we speak about the sanctification of man and his life in Christ. It suffices also because the concept of the redemptive value of Christ's death is still alive among Christian people today. It is different with Paul's teaching on Christ's resurrection. We all know that Easter, the great feast of Jesus' resurrection from the dead, is the principal feast of the ecclesiastical year. But few are able to tell why this is so. Indeed the greater part, if they are honest, would readily admit that Christmas is much dearer to them. This is due to the fact that Western Christianity, much to the detriment of its vitality and joyfulness, has to a great extent lost the awareness of Christ's resurrection as a *redemptive* factor. Reflection upon Paul's epistles and upon the liturgy will help restore proper appreciation.

Christ's death is a vicarious reparation for sin, but it is also the introduction of a new life in which the relationships between God and humanity are changed. The risen Christ is the cornerstone of this new order of salvation; the risen and living Christ is the pivotal point here as well as in all things.

Christ's resurrection (as well as that of every Christian) occupies an important place in the preaching of the Apostle, and is treated by him from many aspects.

As an historical incident, the Lord's resurrection is the basis for, and the starting point of, the apostolic preaching, the great proof of the divine mission of the Redeemer. God raised up Jesus of Nazareth from the dead and exalted Him on His right hand as Leader and Redeemer. Of this the apostles are the joyful witnesses and the divinely appointed heralds (Acts 5:31). From the very first Easter morning this victorious cry, "Christ has risen," has resounded unceasingly (Lk. 24:34). It is found throughout the Acts of the Apostles (1:22; 2:24 ff.; 3:12 ff., etc.). Paul himself writes of it. For him the historical fact is undeniable. Christian teaching is not something vague and fanciful. He himself has seen the risen Lord. For this reason he is an apostle as well as the others, notwithstanding his great unworthiness (I Cor. 9:1; 15:8). He begins the forceful exposition of the resurrection in the First Epistle to the Corinthians with a thorough historic-apologetic proof of the reality of this incident (15:3 ff.).

The resurrection of Jesus is the exemplar of our own bodily resurrection. Paul develops this point *ex professo* in the chapter just mentioned because some —perhaps many?—Corinthians denied the resurrection of the body.[4]

---

[4] See especially I Cor. 15:20–22; Acts 26:23, in a speech by Paul; Col. 1:18; I Cor. 1:14; II Cor. 4:14, etc.

Consequently the resurrection of Christ is the type, the figure of our own resurrection from sin which, in baptism by immersion as was customary at that time, is mystically represented by the rising from the water. Particularly renowned is the passage from the Epistle to the Romans, wherein Paul explains this teaching with its practical consequences (Rom. 6:3–11; also Col. 2:12).

Finally, with Jesus' resurrection began His exaltation and glorification above all creatures; with it began His glorious existence and His triumph over sin and death. Already on the first Pentecost day Peter spoke in this fashion (Acts 2:32–36), and in his Epistle to the Romans St. Paul writes: "For to this end Christ died and rose again, that he might be Lord both of the dead and of the living" (Rom. 14:9; also I Cor. 15:25; Eph. 1:20; Phil. 2:9, etc.).

Though all these indications of the truth can readily be obtained from the apostolic writings, yet there are many texts of which the full meaning appears to require a deeper explanation. These ideas apparently do not exhaust the full depth of Paul's teaching on the resurrection of Christ. They seem not even to touch the center of his thought, which summarizes the different aspects and binds them together in the light of a higher unity. This becomes possible to us only as we consider these texts in the entirety of Paul's teaching on the redemption.

Without doubt Jesus' resurrection as well as His death were personal experiences. But they obtain their full significance only when we look at them as experiences of the Redeemer, as redemptive happenings. Christ did not become incarnate, die, and rise for His own sake, but in His capacity as Redeemer.

We have already considered that Christ's incarnation and mortal existence were an *entering into* the unredeemed state of man. His death was the last consequence of this undertaking, but also its definite completion. The life wherein Christ arose is not the same existence which He laid down on the cross. This is a very important truth, which we are inclined to overlook in our reflections on the resurrection. It is precisely the starting point for the Pauline teaching. "For we know that Christ, having risen from the dead, dies now no more, death no longer has dominion over him. For the death that he died, he died to sin once for all, but the life that he lives, he lives unto God" (Rom. 6:9–10). Through His resurrection, the man Christ inaugurated a new existence—namely, that of "the Son of God by power" (Rom. 1:4). He was always Son of God, but as man He did not have this prerogative of being such "in power" during the time of his mortal exist-

51

ence. The reason for this is the free but real "empty-ing," the *kenosis,* of which Paul speaks in Phil. 2:7. We must be mindful of this, that for the man Christ (that is to say, for the Redeemer) the resurrection signifies the transition from the suffering and pas-sible, from the unredeemed state of existence, to the glorious life with God. If we add to this the great principle of solidarity, we will begin to understand what a basic and elementary place the resurrection of Jesus occupies in Paul's teaching on the redemp-tion. It is worth noting that, in his letters, Paul rele-gates Christ's earthly life to the background. It would almost seem that Paul knows Christ only as He appeared to him on the way to Damascus, glorious and exalted, the risen Lord. Of all that pre-cedes the resurrection, only the incarnation and Jesus' death on the cross seem to be worthy of note. His death was necessary to reconcile mankind with the Father and to expiate sin. "For he who is dead is acquitted of sin" (Rom. 6:7). But it is not enough to die to sin. To live in God, to live the divine life of the Spirit is the proper finis of the resurrection. It is precisely for this reason that Christ had to rise again. Even before the resurrection, He personally possessed the fulness of divine life, but not in His role as our living and *life-giving* Head.

Jesus' resurrection and ascension, His glorification

—that is, the state of being freed from time and space—the whole spiritual, "pneumatic," [5] existence of His glorified humanity was a necessary condition that He might be the Head which influences and vivifies the whole body. Such was God's design; and now that it has been revealed to us, we are enabled, in retrospect, to discover in it certain outstanding but connected lines. The Spirit of Jesus could not be sent upon the Church before Christ Himself was "spiritualized," before He Himself had become a life-giving Spirit through His resurrection (I Cor. 15:45), or, as Paul says elsewhere, before "he had been foreordained Son of God by an act of power in keeping with the holiness of his spirit, by resurrection from the dead" (Rom. 1:4). The Christ who suffered and died, who merited the Spirit for us, was essentially bound to the laws of matter and suffering, but placed Himself freely and really under the power of Law and sin. He did not yet irradiate the Spirit, although He was completely filled with It in the very depth of His divine-human existence. "For the Spirit had not yet been given, seeing that Jesus

[5] Pneumatic: spiritual. The word is derived from *pneuma,* spirit, which in Paul's usage signifies the Holy Spirit as divine person, as well as His supernatural graces and gifts in the individual Christian. Hence the word *pneumatic* is more or less equivalent to our term "supernatural." It is not on a par with "immaterial" in a purely idealistic or gnostic sense.

had not yet been glorified," says the Evangelist John of Christ's mortal life (John 7:39). And the Redeemer Himself adds: "It is expedient for you that I depart. For if I do not go, the Advocate will not come to you; but if I go [that is, if I be glorified], I will send him to you" (John 16:7).

For the Spirit which the faithful receive and which vitalizes us is not any spirit whatsoever, but the *Spirit of Jesus.* The glorified Christ lives in His followers through His Spirit, with whom, in a certain sense, He is identified. This identification is apparent from a profound passage in the Epistle to the Romans: "You, however, are not carnal but spiritual, if indeed the *Spirit of God* dwells within you. But if anyone does not have the *Spirit of Christ,* he does not belong to Christ. But if *Christ* is in you, the body, it is true, is dead by reason of sin, but the spirit is life by reason of justification" (Rom. 8:9–11). Jesus lives spiritually (pneumatically) in His followers. This was not possible before His death and resurrection. He did not even permit the divine life to develop itself completely in His own person, though He could have done so by making His body immortal and glorious and His soul perfectly blessed. Only through His resurrection did He become the Giver of the Spirit and of life, the *life-giving* Life of the members of His mystical body.

Only after His resurrection did He begin the state of life-giving Spirit. Only then was His humanity spiritualized and divinized in such a manner that it became the instrument of the divinity for our sanctification, the channel which gives the Spirit in such a manner that it is Christ's Spirit which dwells in us and sanctifies us.

All this Paul tells us in the short phrase: "[Christ] was delivered up for our sins, and rose again for our justification" (Rom. 4:25).

This is, consequently, the redemptive value of Jesus' resurrection. Through His glorification, His humanity becomes a source of the Spirit for us, that is to say, of eternal life. There are many other texts treating of this truth.

Because He is the Head of all of us, we have already risen and been glorified with Him, in principle, on the first Easter morning. As soon as the individual enters into communion with the glorified Christ through faith and baptism, he begins to participate in that Spirit and that Life; he becomes a part of that coming age,[6] which, in Christ's glorious

[6] Age: a particular period of time in the history of man. *Age* is more specific and definite than *era;* it is commonly used of a period dominated by some central figure or clearly marked feature. Paul speaks frequently of "this, or the present age" and of the "coming age." By the former he means the period and state of affairs of unredeemed mankind; by the latter, the period and condition of redeemed humanity. This new age was inaugurated by Christ's resurrection.

body and glorified soul, has interrupted the vicious circle of fallen mankind. As through one man sin entered into the world and through sin death, so also through one man the vicious circle of doom is broken.

This wonderful teaching of Paul on Christ's resurrection, only briefly outlined here, has not been lost in the teaching of the Church and her liturgical life. Thus we read in the preface of Easter: "Through His death, Christ has overcome our death and through His resurrection He has restored our life." Still, this teaching has become obscure in the consciousness of the faithful through lack of proper instruction. Such a deficiency has its root in our present-day theology, which indeed does not deny this truth, but does not use it to full advantage. Instead, during the past century, it has exhausted itself in the fruitless refutation of all sorts of theological systems which deny the fact of Christ's resurrection. This is not the first time that a well-founded reaction against some heresy has led, not indeed to the opposite error, but at least to the ignoring of that part of the truth which was not denied by the heresy.

It is hoped that the renewed interest in the Bible and the universal and more intense participation in the Church's liturgy will again render us susceptible to the salutary influence of this truly traditional

Christian teaching. Then will the joyous shout "Christ is risen" acquire the same full connotation for our people which it has always had for Eastern Christendom and which we hope it will never lose.

CHAPTER THREE

Conversion to Christ

OW DOES SINFUL, LOST MAN OB-
tain part in the resurrection of Christ? By what
means does he share in the reconciliation of the
world with the Father, in the reconciliation which
the blood of Christ accomplished? How does he
enter into community of life with the risen Christ,
who has become life-giving Spirit and who possesses
the *Pneuma* fully for all who belong to Him? In one
word, how is the individual man actually justified?

This is the way Paul looks at it. God calls a man
to faith through the proclamation of the gospel. As
soon as a person becomes aware of the apostolic

preaching and accepts the glad tidings, he believes
above all in the redemption as it was decreed by
God and as it was accomplished in the man Christ;
he believes in the conciliatory power of Jesus' death
on the cross; he permits himself to be baptized, that
is to say, he receives "the sacrament of faith," which
brings him into contact with Christ and incorporates
him into the Church, His mystical body; through
baptism his sins are forgiven; he receives the Spirit
and is adopted as a child of God. He is now "in
Christ." He has now become a part, even though not
perfectly, of the new age which began with Jesus'
glorification. This whole process Paul calls justification.

I. *The Standard of Perfection*

In this transition from the state of irredemption
to the state of Christian existence, both God and
man play their role. On God's part there is vocation;
and on man's part, faith and baptism. As objective
factors one might also point to the gospel, to the
apostolic preaching and, of course, to the redemption through Jesus' death and resurrection.

It is well to note one thing beforehand. The
Christians to whom St. Paul wrote were, for the most
part, people who had been converted, as adults, from
paganism to Christ—which means that they had not

been handed Christianity on the silver platter of birth and training. It was the first generation of the Church from paganism. Their becoming Christians brought such drastic consequences with it that it meant a complete rupture with the society in which they lived. Not that they were persecuted because of their worship, at least not at that time. In Paul's day—certainly in the period preceding his first Roman imprisonment—Christianity had not yet attracted the public eye. If people were at all aware of its existence, it was looked upon as a type of Judaism. And Jews were to be found all over the Roman Empire. It may also have been considered as one of the many religious cults which were imported from the East and which found small groups of zealous followers almost everywhere. However, Christianity would not tolerate a number of things which everyone considered quite ordinary and which seemed indispensable even in public life. It is almost impossible for us, who live in our material and specialized society, where the natural unity of life is wanting and where politics, art, worship, morals and economics are neatly set side by side as so many separate departments, to imagine how much the worship of divinity penetrated the life of the state, the city and the family in antiquity, and in pagan antiquity. For example, much of the meat which was sold in the market place had its origin in pagan sacrifices. A Jew shuddered at having to touch it. Paul, too, had to deal with matters of conscience on this point (I Cor. 8). This is just one example out of many. To hold an office or to represent some official position was impossible without idolatry for Jews or Christians. The latter soon found themselves forced into a position of juridical and social ostracism. We may imagine how difficult and how dangerous such a condition was; for the absolute power of the state is not an invention of Hitler or Lenin: a person did not have to be a prophet to foresee that Christianity was to have a hard time of it, unless it perished quickly.

Moreover, there were *inexorable demands* in the matter of morals. We must not forget that we are living in a world which, to say the least, was once Christian, and which, when it really comes down to it, still professes moral principles that have their origin in Christianity. But Paul set his foot into a completely pagan world, in which even the theories on morals had long since been thoroughly corrupted. We need only think of the manner in which many philosophers approved of homosexuality and even glorified it as a very sublime form of *eros*. That is precisely the reprimand which Paul gives in his summarization in the Epistle to the Romans (1:32):

"Although they have known the ordinance of God, they have not understood that those who practice such things are deserving of death. And not only do they do these things, but they *applaud* others doing them."

The practice was all of a piece with the rest of their living. This can be noticed, for example, in the two epistles to the Corinthians which have remained. Corinth was a harbor city with a colorful mixture of races and tongues and cults. All of these cults tolerated each other in brotherly fashion, with the same total depravity and shamelessness of morals as now exists in Port Said and Suez, for example. The city was notorious even in antiquity, and the phrases "to go to Corinth" or "to live in Corinthian fashion" were used to insinuate all sorts of free escapades. Perhaps the pessimist is inclined to think that the moral standards of today are not a bit higher. He may be right, for all that—at least from the purely materialistic or quantitative point of view. Yet there are some things which are no longer practiced in our times, at least not in so perverse a manner. Prostitution is not given a religious tone, as it was in Corinth, where thousands of official temple-maids practiced the cult of Venus, in Asiatic manner, for transient sailors. Let it be granted that in the world at large today impurity is hardly considered as sin, but rather as a hygienic and social problem; yet it is not looked upon as a form of cult, as was frequently the case in antiquity.

The Apostle had bidden his followers in Corinth to avoid certain public sinners and givers of scandal. They had not well understood this point. "For," he says (I Cor. 5:9 ff.), "I wrote to you in the letter not to associate with the immoral—not meaning, of course, the immoral of this world, or the covetous, or the greedy, or idolators; otherwise you would have to leave the world. But now I write to you not to associate with one who is called a brother, if he is immoral, or covetous, or an idolator, or evil-tongued, or a drunkard, or greedy." Of what sort they were formerly and could always become again, is indicated in another passage (6:10–11): "Do not err; neither fornicators, nor idolators, nor adulterers, nor the effeminate, nor sodomites, nor thieves, nor the covetous, nor drunkards, nor the evil-tongued, nor the greedy will possess the kingdom of God. And such were some of you, but you have been washed, you have been sanctified, you have been justified." And such were *some* of you. Paul expresses himself considerately. For undoubtedly the greater number of them had been idolators. And as for the rest, they appeared to be anything but angels, even after their conversion.

These are the kinds of happenings which we must vividly keep in mind if we wish to understand at all what a tremendous step those persons took when they became Christians. Whoever descended into the baptismal font as an adult literally left his past life outside with his clothing. It was really a new start! "If anybody is in Christ, he is a new creature," Paul shouts triumphantly. But it was that kind of newness which rent the old wineskins asunder. Whoever had put on Christ looked upon the gear of his former life as rubbish, just as Paul himself, for the sake of Christ, called the privileges and the honor of his Jewish days "loss" (Phil. 3:8). To him, as to the rest, the transition meant a rupture with the past and a marvel of newness.

From all this we can begin to understand why conversion to Christ and all that goes with it occupies such an important place in Paul's epistles. Possibly, many a man and woman, though fully grateful for the privilege of having been *born in the Church,* may feel a touch of envy toward those for whom baptism was *the great experience* in their conscious and adult lives.

II. *In Christ Jesus*

Now we are also in a position to understand why the Apostle places so much stress on *faith,* even more than on baptism. For it is only through a personal and firm faith, that the adult, who is outside the Church, is led to baptism, which incorporates him into Christ. The notion of faith in St. Paul! If only we were able to write on this matter as is fitting. There are few things in his meaningful letters which are so significant even for us and which have retained such a *practical* importance as this particular point. Paul does not understand faith exactly as we do. It is important to note this well. There is not question of a different teaching, but rather of different terminology. By religious faith we mean that the Catholic accepts, on the authority of God, the revealed truths which are proposed to him by the Church. For he believes that the Church has been founded by Christ and is governed by His Spirit. By faith Paul understands the same, but often includes even more. It is not as though faith meant only confidence for Paul. Even the so-called intellectual element which consists in the acceptance of certain *truths* by the *reason* is always included or at least presupposed. For Paul, faith consists primarily in the acceptance of the gospel, that is, of the apostolic preaching of the joyful message. The Christian and the catechumen accept the word of the apostles not as the word of man, but as the message of *God*, which comes to them with authenticity and authority

(I Thess. 1:3–10; I Cor. 5:2; Eph. 1:13, etc.). The
fact is that faith usually arises through hearing. Paul
asserts this in a noteworthy chain of reasonings in
Romans 10:14–21: "For whoever calls upon the
name of the Lord shall be saved"—that is, whoever
calls upon the name of Christ with faith shall be
saved. "How then are they to call upon him in
whom they have not believed? But how are they to
believe in him, of whom they have not heard? And
how are they to hear, if no one preaches? And how
are men to preach unless they be sent? . . . Faith
then depends on hearing and hearing on the word of
Christ," on the preaching on Christ which is done
under His authorization. For faith does not arise
from rumors about Christ, from ordinary news re-
ports, from hearsay evidence, but from the authori-
tative preaching of those who have been sent by
Christ: the apostles, their associates and their
followers.

Even then, faith does not arise by itself. The man
who hears must want to understand. Faith always
remains a free act. It is not without reason that Paul
frequently speaks of the obedience of faith (Rom.
1:5; 16:26; II Cor. 10:5–6). Obedience, real inner
obedience, cannot be forced. Faith does not arise
from the internal evidence of the things one understands oneself. For then it is no longer faith, accept-

67

ance upon authority, but rather understanding or perception or science or sheer deduction (II Cor. 5:7; Hebr.11:1).

Even the man who *wishes* to believe, *cannot* always do so then and there. Paul was the first to teach expressly that faith is a gift of God (Eph. 2:8). This is why the preaching of the glad tidings is laden with power (I Thess. 1:5). The gospel itself is divine energy (Rom. 1:17). Oratorical abilities, style, and such things have basically nothing to do with it. When Paul arrived at Corinth for the first time, he had but recently experienced a setback at Athens, but he had also learned a lesson. On the Areopagus there, the customary meeting place of the intellectual elite of a city which had still preserved many of its ancient glories even though they were mostly pretentious, Paul had tried to introduce his message with a tactful approach and with words of human wisdom. He began his speech with a few rather stoic generalities about the one God. He even quoted a few poets. It was his plan cautiously to prepare the way for what he really had to preach: Christ, who had died and risen again because of the sins of man, Greeks included. However, at the very first sound of the truly Christian content all interest suddenly vanished. His listeners had a fine sense for such matters; they were not easily fooled. A few were at least polite and said: "We will hear thee again on this matter." Others began to ridicule him openly. The idea of a real resurrection was simply too absurd (Acts 17:22–34).

Paul did not use this manner of approach a second time.[1] Arriving at Corinth shortly afterwards, a place where, together with moral depravity, there existed also cultural snobbishness, he proceeded differently. He himself describes his approach (I Cor. 2:1–5): "And I, brethren, when I came to you, did not come with pretentious speech or wisdom, announcing unto you the witness to Christ. For I determined *not to know anything among you, except Jesus Christ and him crucified.* And I was with you in weakness and in fear and in much trembling. And my speech and my preaching were not in the persuasive words of wisdom, but in the demonstration of the Spirit and of power, that your faith might rest, not on the wisdom of men, but on the power of God."

By Spirit and power he does not mean his own personal power of will nor the strength of his own character, but a supernatural efficacy which is given to his words, insofar as they are purely the message

[1] At least not to the same extent or in the same manner, as far as we can ascertain. In his pastoral epistles we can definitely detect a trace of adaptation to Greek culture and mannerisms, but nothing quite like that about which we read in Acts 17.

of the unpretentious, naked cross, without any extra trimmings. This internal power is also given to his words by the Spirit of God, insofar as He is operative in the hearts of those who hear them.

What does a person believe, who is thus led to faith through the cooperation of God's grace, free will, and apostolic preaching? The answer is simple. He believes the gospel which is preached to him (Rom. 1:17, etc.). What did this gospel contain? No pet theories of Paul, but the ordinary early Christian creed, which is still taught to our children today, and of which the first groping attempt at formulation may already be read in I Cor. 15:1–5: "Now, I recall to your minds, brethren, the gospel that I preached to you, which also you received, wherein also you stand, through which also you are being saved, if you hold fast, as I preached it to you —unless you have believed to no purpose. *For I delivered to you first of all what I also received,* that Christ died for our sins according to the Scriptures, and that he was buried, and that he rose again the third day, according to the Scripture, and that he appeared to Cephas, and after that to the Eleven."

That is precisely what will save them, if they persevere therein: faith in Jesus, who died for our sins and rose again from the dead according to the Scriptures. In other words, a person must believe in what we have termed the *redemption in Christ.* He must believe that "God has reconciled the world to himself through Christ" (II Cor. 5:19). Justice will be credited to him, as it was to Abraham, if only he believes in "him, who raised Jesus our Lord from the dead" (Rom. 4:24). Paul writes very simply to the unpretending Macedonians in the first chapter of his very first epistle (but note how characteristic and fundamentally Christian these truths are): "You turned to God from idols, to serve the living and true God, and to await from heaven Jesus, his Son, whom he raised from the dead, who has delivered us from the wrath to come" (I Thess. 1:9–10).

Thus Paul can also say that the man who is justified believes in *God,* not in the sense that he believes in the one or other abstract idea of the Divinity, *le Dieu des philosophes* (the philosophers' God) of Pascal, but that he truly believes in the living and personal active God, the God of Abraham, the God of Isaac, the God of Jacob, who has fulfilled His age-old promises in Christ. The Christian believes in God, active and redemptive through Jesus; in God, who, through Christ, intervenes in the earthly order of things. To sum it up: he believes in the cross. And none of the rulers of this world have known this mystery, says Paul, "for had they known it, they would never have crucified the Lord of glory" (I Cor. 2:8). The Christian also believes that God is operative in every person who believes that God wants to save the world through the cross. Moreover, he believes that God is capable, and has the intention, of justifying the godless for the sake of the blood of Jesus (Rom. 3:25, etc.). Finally he believes in God's activity in His Church, which is the body and the fulness of the glorified Christ and is filled with His power.

Thus we see that in the writings of Paul faith has a definite content which one may reasonably hope to point out by means of precise concepts and judgments. Faith has a definite relationship to the gospel, for the gospel is the glad tidings. Preaching belongs to the very essence of Christianity, and preaching is not possible unless the messengers (Jesus Himself and His apostles above all) use human language and human concepts to express the reality which is being revealed to us. Faith does not mean primarily to feel or to sense, but to hear, understand, and accept. This believing acceptance of the redemption in Christ, as it was preached in the (oral) gospel by the apostles, is precisely what Paul understands by "faith"; and no one will dare deny that this has something to do with the rational and intellectual power of man.

72

Yet this is not the whole picture. Naturally not.
A person does not accept the message of Jesus' death
on the cross in the same manner as a layman believes the report that radar contact has been established with the moon. The gospel does not come to
a man as a piece of news, but as a positive demand
from God. Viewed from the part of man, to believe
means *to enter into the world of God.* And this is
by no means a world of fables, but of reality as
bright and as clear as crystal. Through the act of
faith, which is produced by a wondrous coordination
of divine operation and human volition, man is
thrust into a state of receptivity toward God. Justifying faith is only a beginning, but it is a real beginning; man is brought into contact with the reality of
God, who, through Jesus' death and resurrection,
forced His way into the circle of irredemption.
Everything proceeds from God and must so proceed.
God sent His Son in the flesh. In Christ's humanity
sin is overcome; in His glorification, God prepared
for us the source of eternal life. The circle has been
broken; victory has been obtained. Now God dis-
patches His apostles with the glad tidings: in the
Lord is salvation; whoever calls upon His name shall
be saved.

The first condition is that men *accept* this way
which has been determined by God—the cross of

73

Jesus, which is the only way leading out of their misery. The first condition, then, is that men must *believe*. If one follows this condition through to all its consequences (as Paul frequently does), he will see that it is also the *last* condition, that it is all-embracing. Indeed, does not a complete acceptance of divine redemption include everything? It is not merely what we today like to term "faith"—an acceptance by the intellect that things are such as they have been revealed by God. No, it is not merely that, although that too is quite a bit. It is more: an ever-increasing *desire* for redemption that is founded on the glad tidings, a desire to be taken up into the cycle of redemption, a *response* to the beckoning of God, which is contained in the glad tidings. It is an *obedience* to the will of God, which has been manifested in the redemption (Rom: 1:5; 16:26; II Cor. 10:5; Acts 6:7; Rom. 6:17). It is an absolute *confidence* in God, that He will keep His promises, that His omnipotence will complete in us what He has begun in Christ; a confidence likewise in the blood of Jesus, wherewith we have been redeemed. To sum it up in one phrase: in Paul's mind, perfect faith includes the *surrender* of the entire man—his reason, his emotions, his capacity for acting and suffering— to Christ. For him faith is the motto of the new order in Christ, the characteristic mark of the truly Christian life (Rom. 3:27; Gal. 3:7, etc.).[2]

In the Apostle's view, faith, or, to put it better, *the believing attitude of the soul* toward God, remains the determining element of the Christian life even after conversion. This is partly due to Paul's own experience, to his past life as a Pharisee, and to his continuous strife with the Judaizers.

These adversaries of Paul's were of the opinion that even the Christian, the person who has believed in Jesus and has been baptized in His name, could not be saved without observing the Jewish Law. Faith in Jesus was not sufficient. Jesus Himself was not sufficient. A person could be saved only through the observance of the Law. God wanted it so; the Law was the perfect and eternally valid expression of His will. Justification was, in their opinion, something which a person accomplished himself and by

[2] Thus one sees that in Paul's writings "faith" can signify various things (though it does not always actually refer to all of them) which we are accustomed to indicate by different terms, as, for instance: hope, confidence, subjection, and even love. Hence it is necessary and of great importance to note that the concept of faith of Catholic theology *does not coincide entirely* with that of Paul, even though it does so to a very great extent. Consequently, the terminology of Catholic theology does not coincide with that of many Protestants, insofar as the latter employ the terminology of Paul. This does not mean that there is discord with the teaching of the Apostle, but only that there is a difference in terminology. Any honest person must acknowledge this difference and thus prevent confusion and misunderstanding.

himself, an achievement of the individual himself; and thus, having its origin in his own free activity, it was also to be credited to him as merit, as a reward, as "self-justification." God had to acknowledge it at the time of death or at the last judgment; in their opinion this constituted justification. A person was never really sure of his justification before this solemn declaration of God—a fact which creates a certain state of anxiety in life. In heaven there was strict computation, but no more than that. Man was master of his own destiny. Jesus' death had nothing to do with it, nor had the Spirit. They did not acknowledge original sin, and maintained that man had within himself all necessary faculties to bring about his own salvation. God had given the Law, and that was a precious gift; but after that, a person was on his own and was capable of taking care of himself. That is what was meant by their dictum: "Man is justified through the works of the Law." Thus one sees that the ever-recurring human element of their system was nothing but spiritual self-sufficiency, pride.

Here Paul voices a vehement and angry denial. This interpretation cuts at the essence of Christianity in the name of piety. It has no idea whatever of the divine economy of salvation and is further removed from the cross of Jesus than is paganism itself.

"Man is *not* justified by the works of the Law, but by faith." Man cannot keep the Law by his own power, and the Law does not give him the power to do so; nor are the divine promises, the only source of salvation, connected with the Law. The Law is only a temporary arrangement, whose function consists in the multiplication of trespasses and has already been considered.

The most profound reason for Paul's vehement reaction against the Judaizers, however, is that they want to attribute to man the honor which belongs to God alone. Self-justification becomes the basis for self-boasting, the *kauchesis,* which Paul utterly detests because it detracts from the glory of God. All men are sinners, powerless, and can only be saved through the blood of the Lamb, that is, through the *divine* order of salvation, through the redemption that has its origin in *God.* Faith is the disposition of the soul whereby it acknowledges this order instituted by God. Hence Paul sings the praises of faith, even more than those of charity. For faith renders all honor and glory to God alone and not to man. Faith is no "personal work," no accomplishment of the individual. Naturally, it is an act, much more powerful and comprehensive than any work of the Law regardless of its character, for it means the change of the whole man and begins with

77

his innermost being. The Pharisaical observance of the Law, on the contrary, has its origin as well as its finis in man himself; it in nowise breaks through the circle of damnation. And yet, faith also truly has its starting point in man (even though not from man alone), but it *does not have its final resting point in man himself*. The cleavage which it opens toward God is not again closed. Through faith we acknowledge that we are sinners and dead; that God has power to reawaken us to life through the death of Jesus; and that when the time comes He will also raise us from the dead with Him. It is only after we view Christ's death on the cross through the eyes of faith, and not with the eyes of the rulers of this world (I Cor. 2:8), that we become aware of what great sinners we really are. It is only after we believe in Jesus' resurrection, that we begin to acknowledge the life-giving power of God, in comparison with which all human powers are a farce. Faith gives honor to God.

Would you like to know how Paul pictures the power and the purity of Christian faith? Then read Rom. 4:17–25. And as you begin to read the text, do not think that, because it deals with Abraham, it is some antiquated passage with no import for us. The Jews always had Abraham upon their tongues, and Paul here describes him on the basis of Old

Testament texts. Yet he also presents Abraham as a type of the believing Christian, the "father of our faith," as he is designated in our liturgy. For his starting point, Paul draws upon the account in Genesis where we are told that God promised Abraham a son of his own body and a multitudinous progeny—all of which seemed hopelessly impossible, since Abraham himself was now an old man and his wife Sara had always been sterile. Then note how Paul describes the characteristics of this faith and how he draws from it the outline of the Christian belief in the resurrection. "Abraham . . . is the father of us all, as it is written, 'I have appointed thee the father of many nations.' He is our father in the sight of God, whom he believed, who gives life to the dead and calls things that are not as though they were. Abraham hoping against hope believed, so that he became the father of many nations, according to what was said, 'So shall thy offspring be.' And without weakening in faith, he considered his own deadened body (for he was almost a hundred years old) and the deadened womb of Sara; and yet in view of the promises of God, he did not waver through unbelief but was strengthened in faith, *giving glory to God,* being fully aware that whatever God has promised he is able also to perform. Therefore it was credited to him as justice.

79

Now not for his sake only was it written that 'It was credited to him,' but for the sake of us also, to whom it will be credited if we believe in him who raised Jesus our Lord from the dead" (Rom. 4:17–24).

On the strength of God's word alone Abraham expected what was humanly impossible. By doing so he gave glory to God; by doing so he looked upon God *as God* and not as man—though it were the best and the most powerful among men. He confidently expected from God not only what was humanly possible, be it the loftiest of possibilities—but a miracle in the concrete reality of his own life, not one far off in time and space.

Even more expressive and of greater import is the passage in I Cor. 1:17–31, which reveals the necessary bond between faith and suffering. In this passage Paul explains to the Corinthians why he had brought them the glad tidings under the particular aspect he had chosen, as the announcement of the crucified Christ. This manner of presentation was not a question of mere tactics, but was demanded by the very nature of the matter itself. "For Christ . . . [sent me] . . . to preach the gospel, not with wisdom of words, lest the cross of Christ be made void. For the doctrine of the cross is foolishness to those who perish, but to those who are saved, that is, to us, it is the power of God. For it is written, 'I will destroy the wisdom of the wise, and the prudence of the prudent I will reject.' Where is the 'wise man'? Where is the scribe? Where is the disputant of this world? Has not God turned to foolishness the 'wisdom' of this world? For since, in God's wisdom, the world did not come to know God by 'wisdom,' it pleased God, by the foolishness of our preaching, to save *those who believe*. For the Jews ask for signs, and the Greeks look for 'wisdom'; but we, for our part, preach a crucified Christ—to the Jews indeed a stumbling-block and to the Gentiles foolishness, but to those who are called, both Jews and Greeks, Christ, the power of God and the wisdom of God. For the foolishness of God is wiser than men, and the weakness of God stronger than men. For consider your own call, brethren: that there were not many wise according to the flesh, not many mighty, not many noble. But . . . the weak things of the world has God chosen to put to shame the strong, and the base things of the world and the despised has God chosen, and the things that are not, to bring to naught the things that are; *lest any flesh should pride itself before him.* From him you are in Christ Jesus, who has become for us God-given wisdom, and justice, and sanctification, and redemption; so that, just as it is written, 'Let him who takes pride, *take pride in the Lord.'* "

Even here we notice the extreme care which he had for the glory of God. This is safeguarded only through faith in the cross. The message of the cross (which is to say, the gospel: the news that God saves the world through the cross and through a man who was cruelly and shamefully put to death), this is foolishness to the Greek mentality, the purely human mentality, and a stumbling-block for Jewish pride, human pride. It is, however, the manner in which God actually operates. This weakness and foolishness is the weakness and the foolishness of *God;* in other words, it is a superior force that manifests and unfolds itself in human life.

Again we stumble upon the *modus suprahumanus,* the superhuman manner and requirement of faith. God justifies the godless (Rom. 4:4). God raises the dead to life, and calls into existence that which was not (Rom. 4:17; I Cor. 1:28). God saves through the cross, through that which is weakness and foolishness (I Cor. 1:17–25). All this adds up to the reality and, at the same time, to the ineffability of God. By faith we accept both to the utmost. For this reason faith is the great force of a Christian life.

This requirement—that our faith accept what is entirely divine in a *practical* manner—applies also to us. Faith, in the concrete divine order of salvation, always includes one or more points which demand real submission to divine revelation on the part of the human spirit, contrary to all human evidence and appearances. It comprises things which we believe only on the authority of God, precisely because He is God. That is how we render Him honor. These points are not always the same for all persons. In Paul's time and surroundings the resurrection constituted a crisis of faith: the Greek mentality was ready to accept such an occurrence merely as a myth, but not as the actual case of a Jew who was crucified some twenty-five years ago in a remote corner of the civilized world. We have become too accustomed to the idea of resurrection; furthermore, the very fact of the resurrection is too distant from our times. We have also become accustomed to honor the cross of Christ, at least in our own surroundings: we hardly think of the cross as an instrument of ignominious execution. But the critical difficulty for faith will always appear in one form or another. In our time it may perhaps be the Church or one of its characteristics. Is that organization of men, at times all too human, of institutions, customs, and devotions, really the society which was intended by God and filled with Christ's saving powers, outside of which salvation for mankind is impossible? Or take another point. We are well aware that God's will is absolute; we even acknowledge the fact with edifying words in our conversation with others. Suddenly, by the inscrutable will of God there occurs a drastic interference in our own lives. Then we are no longer able to discern His will. What happens to our faith in the divine providence? This is the same as asking what happens to our faith in the manner in which God actually deals with us.

Faith means *to live God* within ourselves, within our own being; to see and receive the divine super-reality into our existence and into our own world. It is a divine illumination of reality, not an idealistic subterfuge, not an escape from reality. It is a leap into complete reality and hence into the yet unknown. It is a seizing of the Hand one does not see.

III. *The Spirit*

The notion of faith according to the mind of Paul has occupied us too long to be able to give sufficient attention to his teaching on *baptism*. Only "he who believes and is baptized shall be saved" (Mk. 16: 16). Baptism is the sacrament of faith, and, from the very first, baptism and profession of faith have been associated with one another. The first real consequence of a person's faith in Christ is that he permits himself to be baptized. Through baptism he becomes a member of Christ and his justification is completed. "Do you not know," asks Paul of the Romans (meaning: Of course, you know), "that all we who have been baptized into Christ Jesus have been baptized into his death? For we were buried with him by means of baptism into death, in order that, just as Christ has arisen from the dead through the glory of the Father, so we also may walk in the newness of life" (Rom. 6:3–4). And to the Galatians he writes briefly but pointedly: "For all you who have been baptized into Christ, have put on Christ" (Gal. 3:27). By baptism a man is consecrated and incorporated; he becomes a member of that mystical, but nonetheless real, society of death and life which constitutes Christian life. He enters into the state of being a child of God, a sharer of the spirit of Christ. He is now *in Christ*.

This chapter may not be concluded without indicating how, in this whole process of justification, God's initiative and honor are not diminished by the fact that man also plays his part freely. Man does so not only by faith, which renders due honor to God, but much more through something which is above any thought or activity of man. This peculiar something is called *vocation* by Paul. It is really a pity that our manner of speaking restricts the use of this word to the particular instances of vocation to the priesthood or to the convent. Paul is also acquainted with this usage, conscious as he is of his personal vocation as an apostle. This, however, does not hinder him from preferring the word as something indicative of the special status of all Christians, whereby they are all God's beloved, His saints, His specially chosen ones, His elect. God's choice has made them such. By this he means that, in accordance with His eternal decisions, God calls the individual man to the status of a Christian through the preaching of the gospel (II Thess. 2:14). God thus calls him to eternal life (I Tim. 6:12), to His own eternal kingdom, His glory and unsurpassable light (I Thess. 2:12; I Peter 2:9; 5:10). This calling is heavenly (Hebr. 3:1). It comes from and tends toward heaven (Phil. 3:14), even though it now exists in hope (Eph. 1:18; 4:4). The Christian is called into the unity of that one body, as an individual, but not individualistically (Col. 3:15).

Thus it is that this difficult process of conversion to Christ falls entirely under the seal of divine activity. God *calls* His beloved. In the knowledge of this fact, the baptized person may live proudly and securely with the assurance that God, through whom he "has been called into fellowship with his Son, Jesus Christ our Lord" (I Cor. 1:9), is faithful and able to complete His work.

CHAPTER FOUR

Existence in Christ

*N*OW WE ARE READY TO CONSIDER
the complete Christian life as Paul pictures it. It is
possible to evaluate the beautiful and the real only
through comparison with the ugly and the unreal,
and vice versa. That many Catholics have lost all
awareness of the ugly in so many instances of religious art can be explained only by our age of in-
dustrial mass production which never, or at the most
seldom, allows them an opportunity to see the truly
beautiful so that they might make the necessary
comparisons. Whoever can, in his mind's eye, com-
pare ordinary church windows with the beautiful

windows of Chartres, can quickly reach a decision. Or take another example: that Grieg's compositions contain no more than sweet and convenient romanticism becomes clear to us only if we have the ability to recognize the absolute music of Bach and Bartók. Let this suffice.

I. *Divine Sonship*

In like manner we are capable of understanding what true Christian life means only if we know the two opposites with which it contrasts: the state of irredemption and the state of careless indifference. For this reason we first had to learn from the Apostle —that is, God had to tell us—the abysmal misery of man without Christ. We shall understand what redemption in Christ means only when, through God's enlightenment, we are permitted to see from what condition we were freed by Jesus' death and resurrection. Man is inclined to view this condition, the normal state of the unbeliever, as trifling, since he judges merely from externals. Nor is the natural man capable of penetrating this abyss. Only God can tell us what it means to be excluded from His life and grace. Against this gloomy background the splendor of redeemed man comes strongly to the fore. "For you were once darkness, but now you are light in the Lord. Walk, then, as children of light, for the fruit of the light is in all goodness and justice and truth" (Eph. 5:8–9). If now we follow the Apostle in his description of redeemed man, if we hear from his mouth the praise of the glories of the Christian status, we shall again feel a certain inclination to accuse him of exaggeration. The person who judges only by his "ordinary common sense" will find the tableau of the sinner too dark, and that of the Christian too sweet; perhaps he will suspect Paul of that peculiar characteristic of craftsmen which makes them artists, but which the ordinary person finds a bit strange—namely, the ability to portray reality in sharper lines than it normally has in the eyes of most people.

Two things are certain. First, Paul did not belong to that group of idealists who lose all sense of the real. As one peruses his letters, one quickly becomes aware that he has a strong grasp of the world and its dangers, of man and his weaknesses. Neither does he idealize his Christians. He does not, for example, overlook the unpleasant fact that his Corinthian flock is fighting within itself, that it tolerates scandal-mongers, that it is in danger of returning into the characteristic sins of paganism, and that, in cold fact, it does not yet possess a very profound understanding of true Christianity. And yet at the same time he adheres to his Christian ideals. He does not hesitate

89

to present the Christian life in all its *fulness,* with all its glories and all its demands, to these people, who have just come from paganism and are not yet sustained by a Christian education and the tradition of centuries and who are living as a small minority in the midst of idolatry and moral decadence. He does not spare them; he does not compromise; he is not satisfied with a type of stoic moralism, as was then customary. On the contrary, he considers this ideal— this superiority of life and work—as *normal,* as an ordinary Christian ideal. This is the second point to which we wish to call attention. Paul does not acknowledge two kinds of perfection. He does not distinguish between an ideal for the masses and one for a few chosen souls. Indeed, in certain cases he acknowledges the great value of virginity in order to serve God more easily and more exclusively (I Cor. 7). In like manner the gospel gives us the scriptural basis for the so-called evangelical counsels, yet they are only special means toward the attaining of that one great goal, which is the same for all and obligatory on all. In this regard it may be observed that the same truth applies to the Sermon on the Mount: the ideal of the Christian life which the Redeemer Himself presents to us in these chapters of Matthew is generally viewed with admiration, but most Christians think that there is question merely of something which is advised or which is obligatory only on the elite. That opinion is wrong. In His Sermon on the Mount, Jesus presents a program which all true Christians must strive to realize. Furthermore, it has this characteristic of a genuine ideal: that it is never accomplished by the general run of mankind. Yet it is obligatory as an ideal. All God's children are obliged to strive after it, although they are aware that, on this earth, complete justification consists in a hunger and thirst which will be ultimately satisfied only in heaven. Paul likewise regards the Christian life as something momentous and profound. All the same, he knows that the people of his time are weak and sinful, no better than our own generation, nor of a different clay from it. Still he holds before their eyes the complete ideal. He cannot do otherwise. "Woe is me if I do not preach the gospel" with all its entailments. The divine commission of the apostolate which he received leaves him no choice. It is precisely this combination of what we may call idealism and realism that gives his letters an extraordinary vitality and power, and bestows on the Christian status a *peculiar intensity,* which is proper to it wherever and whenever the Christian life is lived fully.

II. *The Fruit of the Spirit*

Before we begin to consider Pauline Christianity as an obligation, as a norm of life and action, we must first know how to view it in its innermost aspect: as a mode of being or existence, a way of life, a principle of life from which all works must flow spontaneously. This constitutes the leading motif of Paul's moral teaching. Just as a plant grows and blooms and bears fruit by its very nature in virtue of its intrinsic life-principle (or, to put it differently, in virtue of itself, simply by being what it is), so also Christian virtues and works of love are viewed as the quasi-natural bloom and result of that new life, which forms us into Christ and which the Christian receives at baptism. For this reason Paul speaks of the *"fruit* of the Spirit" (Gal. 5:22). All the beautiful virtues and works which he describes under this striking image are, as it were, one single fruit which blossoms forth spontaneously from the inner nature of the Spirit given to the Christian. In baptism sinful man receives from God, as from an exterior principle, the Spirit of Christ, which then becomes an interior, supernatural principle of life. If only man lives according to this new "nature," the fruit will not be wanting. For this reason too, Paul adds, the Christian is not subject to the Law. The

Law being an exterior rule of works, whoever truly lives by the Spirit has no need of the Torah. His code of ethics is this: be what you really are; live according to what you have become through God's grace.

How then does the Apostle describe this principle of life, this Christian mode of existence whence all things must flow? In various ways. Among his choice expressions is *"existence in Christ."* This or a similar formula recurs constantly: "in Christ," "in Christ Jesus," "in the Lord." What does it mean? At times it would seem that the words have hardly any special signification whatever. For example, when he writes: "Paul . . . to all the saints in Christ Jesus that are at Philippi" (Phil. 1:1), this means nothing more than if we were to say: "To all the Christians at Philippi." Or take the passage (II Cor. 12:2) in which he gives us the wonderful account of his great mystical experience: "I know a man in Christ who fourteen years ago—whether in the body I do not know, or out of the body I do not know, God knows —such a one was caught up to the third heaven." Does "a man in Christ" mean anything more than a Christian? Perhaps not—especially since Paul never uses the word *Christian*. The word indeed existed in his time, but it seems to have been used only by those outside the Church and probably with a depreciative tone. However, there are many other passages in which the formula "in Christ" has a fuller connotation, and it is from these that we must seek its proper meaning; just as today we do not inquire into the meaning of the word *Catholic* from such expressions as the "Catholic Club" or the "Catholic Bowling Team," but from the words of the Creed, "I believe in the one, holy, catholic, and apostolic church."

Consider, for instance, such a text as this: "Thus do you consider yourselves also as dead to sin, but alive to God *in Christ Jesus*" (Rom. 6:11). Because in some way or other they are one with Christ, they are Christians, dead to sin, living unto God.

Or this: "From him you are in Christ Jesus, who has become for us God-given wisdom, and justice, and redemption" (I Cor. 1:30). Because a person is in Christ, he shares in *His* wisdom and holiness. Thus to be in Christ means to share in Christ's life, and that, because God wills it so.

Ponder this verse: "If then any man is in Christ, he is a new creature" (II Cor. 5:17). Because a man is in Christ, he has received a new life or existence—that is, a different type of life: namely, supernatural. Indeed, everyone knows from experience that the bodily and natural existence remains the same and that by baptism a person does not become more healthy, more capable or more intelligent; thus the

94

proper Christian mode of existence is again empha-
sized as the state of being united with Christ.

One must observe that for Paul the expressions
"I am in Christ" or "Christ is in me" are the same.
We have an example of the latter in the famous
passage from Galatians (2:19–20): "For I through
the Law have died to the Law that I may live to
God. With Christ I am nailed to the cross. It is now
no longer I that live, but Christ lives in me. And the
life that I now live in the flesh, I live in the faith of
the Son of God, who loved me and gave himself up
for me." Does Paul really mean to say that once he
became a Christian he no longer lived his own life?
Of course not. Moreover, he himself immediately
clarifies this when he adds: "And the life that I now
live in the flesh I live in the faith of the Son of
God." Thus it is Paul himself who is living. However, he does wish to say that this present and pro-
visional life in the flesh, this passing state which he
shares with all men, is, as far as he is concerned,
entirely spent in faith in Christ. It is this point which
puts a meaning into things. And for this reason,
Christ lives in him. We know that, for Paul, "to
believe," in its full meaning, signifies surrender to
God in Christ. This is the desire he expresses to the
Ephesians: "May Christ dwell through faith in your
hearts" (Eph. 3:17). Here we have an explanation

95

of the formula "in Christ" and of its inverse, "Christ in us": through faith and love we are united to the Lord. Because our thoughts are filled with Him, and our hearts and our wills are firmly surrendered to Him, He remains in us by a spiritual presence, just as the lover lives in his beloved even when absent. I do not say that Paul's expression "in Christ" means no more, but it does mean at least this much.

Indeed, it means much more. We have no right to reduce this existence "in Christ" merely to some sort of psychological actuality, no matter how refined it may be. Christ is in man through the Spirit, who lives in the believer. The Spirit occupies an important role in Paul's letters, where the word *pneuma* (spirit) occurs no less than one hundred and forty-six times. We wish now to speak only of the Spirit of God, or the Spirit of Christ, as it is shared with the believers, according to Paul's teaching. We have already seen that there is a close interrelation between the glorified Saviour and the Spirit. The same holds true here. Without distinguishing, Paul speaks of being justified in Christ (Gal. 2:17) or in the Spirit (I Cor. 6:11), and of being sanctified in Christ or in the Spirit (Eph. 4:30).

In baptism the believer receives the Holy Spirit and His gifts. "The charity of God is poured forth in our

heart by the Holy Spirit who has been given to us"
(Rom. 5:5). This Spirit of God dwells permanently
in the Christian; it is He who, through His gifts and
graces, gives us new life, the Christian "existence,"
and who renders us conformable to Christ—all because Jesus has merited the Spirit for us by His
death, and because the glorified Saviour, sitting at
the right hand of God, sends this Spirit into the
believer. For this reason the Spirit renders us conformable to the image of the Only-Begotten, who is
the first-born of many brethren (Rom. 8:29). "For
whoever are led by the Spirit of God, they are the
sons of God. Now you have not received a spirit of
bondage so as to be again in fear, but you have
received a spirit of adoption as sons, by virtue of
which we cry, 'Abba! Father!' The Spirit himself
gives testimony to our spirit that we are sons of
God" (Rom. 8:13–16). We can be sons of God only
through union with Christ, the only Son of God.
There is no other way. The Spirit of Jesus, which is
given us, makes us conformable to Him, so that God
can recognize in us the image of His Only-Begotten.
Furthermore, the Spirit also infuses into us the
disposition proper to children: the freedom and the
confidence in the Father, together with the strong,
surpassing desire for the Father, which constitutes
the very essence of the Son, the state of "existing

97

completely in and for the Father." This is the significance of the words: "By virtue of the spirit we cry, 'Abba! Father!' " We do not merely speak, but we cry with a strong and sturdy cry that surges from the depth of the spirit. This, too, is the meaning of the other unforgettable words in the memorable eighth chapter of the Epistle to the Romans which teach a complete theology of prayer: "But in like manner the Spirit also helps our weakness. For we do not know what we should pray for as we ought, but the Spirit himself pleads for us with unutterable groanings. And he who searches the hearts knows what the Spirit desires" (Rom. 8:26–27).

Thus the Spirit makes us children of God. Thus we are in Christ, and Christ is in us, through the Spirit.

III. *Love*

That is how the Apostle sums up the whole Christian life. Man, who was lost and helpless, a slave of sin and of the flesh, the enemy of God and excluded from the blessings of communion with God and from the Messianic promises, is now, through faith and baptism, a child of God, a brother of Christ, endowed with the Spirit, heir of all heavenly glory. He is still living in the flesh. Concupiscence still rages in his members. Death awaits him. But he has received the pledge of the Spirit and he lives in the firm hope that death will be no more than a transition to the state of eternal "existence with Christ," and that, at the second coming of Jesus, his body will rise in glory. "Having been justified therefore by faith, let us have peace with God through our Lord Jesus Christ" (Rom. 5:1).[1]

We must not, however, suppose that the Christian may now take it easy and rest on his laurels. Paul is by no means a quietist. The Christian is not assured of his salvation; he may not cling like a parasite to the vocation and graces he has received from God. He must work and strive and labor with the precious gifts of God in order to increase them a hundred-fold. That is the meaning of the epistle of Septuagesima Sunday (I Cor. 9:24–27; 10:1–5). Only he who exerts himself as Paul did, who denies himself many things while he is *in training*, who expends the

---

[1] The Confraternity of Christian Doctrine edition of the New Testament translates this verse: "Having been justified therefore by faith, let us have peace . . ." This is also the reading of the Vulgate, and of most critical Greek texts. However, many modern translators and commentators prefer to read the indicative *echomen*, in place of the subjunctive *echōmen: we have peace*, in place of *let us have peace*. Thus, Spencer, O.P., *The New Testament*, New York, 1937; Sickenberger, *Die Briefe des heiligen Paulus an die Korinthier und Römer*, Bonn, 1932; Viard, O.P., *Epître Aux Romains*, Paris, 1949. According to the latter, this is also the admitted reading of the seventeenth edition (1941) of Nestle.—Tr.

utmost strength in the arena to win the prize, may regard himself as a real Christian. "Do you not know that those who run in a race, all indeed run, but one receives the prize? So run as to obtain it. And everyone in a contest abstains from all things—and they indeed to receive a perishable crown, but we an imperishable" (I Cor. 9:24–25).

And in the Second Epistle to the Corinthians he writes: "Yes, working together with him we entreat you not to receive the grace of God in vain. For he says, 'In an acceptable time I have heard thee, and in the day of salvation I have helped thee.' Behold now is the acceptable time; behold now is the day of salvation" (6:1–2).

To the Ephesians: "See to it therefore, brethren, that you walk with care: not as unwise but as wise, making the most of your time, because the days are evil. Therefore do not become foolish, but understand what the will of the Lord is" (5:15–17).

The fruit of the Spirit is charity. As Paul says elsewhere in the same epistle: "For in Christ Jesus neither circumcision is of any avail, nor uncircumcision, but faith which works through charity" (5:6). Charity brings unity into the multiplicity of his admonitions. She is the queen. Her worth far surpasses even the most brilliant manifestations of a charismatic [2] spirit, which frequently occurred in the early Church and which were often anxiously sought after by the Christians. "If I should speak with the tongues of men and of angels, but do not have charity, I have become as sounding brass or a tinkling cymbal. And if I have prophecy and know all mysteries and all knowledge, and if I have all faith so as to remove mountains, yet do not have charity, I am nothing" (I Cor. 13:1–3). This is the way he opens his renowned hymn in praise of *charity*. Without doubt, this charity is love of God. Without doubt also, it manifests itself as love of neighbor. Paul would approve the words of St. John: "He who has the goods of this world and sees his brother in need and closes his heart to him, how does the love of God abide in him?" (I John 3:17); or that other passage: "If anyone says 'I love God' and hates his brother, he is a liar. For how can he who does not love his brother, whom he sees, love God, whom he does not see?" (I John 4:19–20). Indeed, Paul himself describes the queen of virtues in the glowing words: "Charity is patient, is kind; charity does not envy, is not pretentious, is not puffed up, is not

[2] Charisms: special graces, given by the Holy Spirit, not so much for the personal sanctification of the individual who received them as for the benefit of the community. These gifts were quite frequent in the early Church, and often had striking forms, such as prophecy, the gift of tongues, power to work miracles, etc.

101

ambitious, is not self-seeking, is not provoked; thinks no evil, does not rejoice over wickedness, but rejoices with the truth; bears with all things, believes all things, hopes all things, endures all things" (I Cor. 13:4–7).

Paul rightly sang the praises of charity in this lyric fashion. Without exaggerating, one may say that Christianity reveals itself to the world through charity, for, as the Master Himself declared (John 13:35), "By this will all men know that you are my disciples, if you have love for one another." The Jew loved only his countryman. The pagan of Paul's time had begun to rise above this old-fashioned restriction, but his charity lacked in purity and disinterestedness what it seemed to have gained through universality. The charity of the Greeks was called *eros;* that of the Christians, *agape.* The newness of Christian charity is indicated most strongly through this new word, which was not familiar to the Greeks. A different word was necessary for a different reality, hitherto unknown—for the *eros* is naturalistic, even in its most idealistic forms, as for instance in Plato's *Symposion.* True, Stoic philosophy taught that all men are equal because all share in the one world spirit; but this pantheistically inclined ideal of humanity was abstract and did not have the power to reform human morals. The power which transforms and reforms man in spite of all his misery and which has not lost its effect even today, is Christian charity. Jesus' death on the cross, which is the supreme revelation of divine charity, has taught man what charity really is. "In this we have come to know his love," writes St. John, "that he laid down his life for us" (I John 3:16). And Paul writes: "Here there is not 'Gentile and Jew,' 'circumcised and uncircumcised,' 'Barbarian and Scythian,' 'slave and freeman'; but Christ is all things and in all" (Col. 3:11). It is not the theoretic conviction that all men share in the same human nature which has brought man to mercy and compassion, but faith in Jesus' own words: "As long as you did it for one of these, the least of my brethren, you did it for me" (Matt. 25:40).

This is the reason why Christian charity, from its very beginning, was not merely an ideal or a noble sentiment, but was practical, efficient, ready to sacrifice itself for a fellow man. The attention of the pagan was drawn by this tangible manifestation which grasped firmly into real life.

For this reason likewise, charity was, from the very first, coupled with works. We are perhaps surprised that Paul writes repeatedly and in detail in many of his epistles about collections. Two chapters of his Second Epistle to the Corinthians are devoted to organizing the collection of money for the poor

103

Christians in Jerusalem. Even at the end of the First Epistle to the Corinthians, he did not consider it beneath his dignity to write: "Now concerning the collection being made for the saints, as I have ordered the churches of Galatia, do you also. On the first day of the week, let each one of you put aside at home and lay up whatever he has a mind to, so that the collections may not have to be made after I have come. But when I am with you, whomever you may authorize by giving credentials, them I will send to carry your gift to Jerusalem. And if it is important enough for me also to go, they shall go with me" (I Cor. 16:1–4).

Paul also drew another conclusion from this principle of charity, which frequently demands a great sacrifice on our part. It is the avoidance of scandal to weaker brothers. The Apostle acknowledges this duty and does not hesitate to impose it even in matters which, considered in themselves, are permissible. Such, for instance, is the question of the *idolothytes,* the meat which was offered to idols. Much of it was sold and used for profane purpose, thus finding its way into the market place and onto the tables of the pagans. As for himself, Paul is totally convinced that one may freely eat it whenever it is used apart from the cult of the idols. Because of their enlightened view of the faith, many Christians thought in like manner; not all, however. There were brethren, says Paul, who did not share this understanding. We would call them narrow-minded people. Because of their old pagan practices, they could not as yet maintain an indifferent point of view, but were of the opinion that they sinned by eating such meat. Theirs was an erroneous conscience, indeed, but one which nonetheless could be the cause of grievous sin. "Still," says the Apostle to the more enlightened, "take care lest perhaps this right of yours become a stumbling block to the weak . . . and through your 'knowledge' the weak one will perish, the brother for whom Christ died. Now when you sin thus against the brethren and wound their weak conscience, you sin against Christ. Therefore, if food scandalizes my brother, I will eat flesh no more forever, lest I scandalize my brother" (I Cor. 8:1–13).

Regarding the community first and foremost, Christian charity is the bond of perfection which binds together the body of Christ. It is the means to unity and the manifestation thereof. For this reason the Eucharist is the sacrament of Christian charity par excellence. It is this not merely because it unites us all with Christ, but especially because it unites us more intimately with each other. "The cup of blessing that we bless, is it not the sharing of the blood of Christ? And the bread we break, is it not the partaking of the body of the Lord? Because the bread is one, we, though many, are one body, all of us who partake of the one bread" (I Cor. 10:16–17).

IV. *Suffering*

We may not end this too brief conspectus of Paul's view of the Christian life without at least a word on that very important factor which played a role not only in his life, but has its part, too, in every life: *suffering*. From his epistles we can learn the Christian viewpoint on unavoidable suffering. Pain was not spared the Apostle, but was his portion in different ways: a mysterious sickness, persecution, anxious solicitude for the tender plants of his churches, the ever-growing desire to be with Christ. At the same time he was sufficiently realistic to recognize that suffering occupies a large place in the life of every individual. For this reason he does not pass it over in silence; he does not ignore the existence of this problem; he does not even try to ignore it stoically. A compassionate person, Paul did not try to hide his feelings. However, his philosophy of suffering is profoundly Christian. He regards it in the first place as a means toward closer conformity with the crucified Christ. One might almost imagine that he is speaking of one of the great suffering mystics of later ages, of a St. Francis of Assisi or a St. Teresa of

106

Avila—"Always bearing about in our body the dying Jesus, so that the life also of Jesus may be made manifest in our bodily frame. For we the living are constantly being handed over to death for Jesus' sake, that the life also of Jesus may be made manifest in our mortal flesh" (II Cor. 4:10–11). Furthermore, the marks of the sufferings and persecutions he endured in the service of the Lord are marks of honor and proof of his special adherence to Christ. "Henceforth let no man give me trouble, for I bear the marks of the Lord Jesus in my body" (Gal. 6:17).

Seen in this light, Christian suffering is not only honorable and a token of authentic Christianity, it is also necessary. And that for two reasons. First, suffering is necessary for the person himself, being a guarantee of future glory, compared to which it appears as nothing and ought not even be mentioned. "But if we are sons, we are heirs also: heirs indeed of God and joint heirs of Christ, provided, however, we suffer with him that we may also be glorified with him. For I reckon that the sufferings of the present time are not worthy to be compared with the glory to come that will be revealed in us" (Rom. 8:17–18). "For our present light affliction, which is for the moment, prepares for us an eternal weight of glory that is beyond all measure" (II Cor. 4:17). Secondly, pain, for which despair or unbelief has no solution, renders yet another service to the Christian.

The natural helplessness and uselessness of a suffering and weak man acquire a real purpose when endured in Christ. "I rejoice now," writes the Apostle from the painful inactivity of his imprisonment, "in the suffering I bear for your sake; and what is lacking of the sufferings of Christ, I fill up in my flesh for his body which is the Church" (Col. 1:24). Christ's suffering is not ended. He suffers in His members, and by means of our sufferings He has deigned to grant the utmost efficacy to His own suffering and death. His passion perpetuates itself to the end of time in the souls of those who suffer together with Him. Jesus will be in agony till the end of the world; hence, this is no time for us to sleep.

Thus a miserable man may rightly say: "I *rejoice* that I may suffer." Thus Paul combines in one sentence, "great tribulation, with joy of the Holy Spirit" (I Thess. 1:6), as though it were the most natural thing in the world. Mind you, he writes in this manner in the very first chapter of his first epistle. Whoever wishes to repeat these things after him—seriously, as an expression of his own life and not as a mere pious formula—must truly be "in Christ" and activated "by the Spirit" and must bear much fruit through the works of an indefatigable "charity."

108

CHAPTER FIVE

The Body of Christ

*O*UR AGE IS CHARACTERIZED BY A
new and exultant feeling of solidarity. The sins of
individualism are severely punished. Everywhere one
perceives a new feeling of solidarity which must
reconcile many old rivalries and heal many old
wounds. In reality, this nostalgia is as old as mankind. We speak of an innate and insuperable desire
for happiness, and in doing so we think mostly of
ourselves; but the longing for a perfect society is
equally strong, since man has remained at least
vaguely conscious that "it is not good for him to be
alone." Augustine described heaven as the perfect

society of the saints. There is a certain common element which unites the aspirations of such widely divergent groups as the Community of the Dead Sea Scrolls, the Anabaptists and other sects with their Messianic dreams, with the firm belief of the Mother Church in the heavenly Jerusalem. This element is constituted by the consciousness that man can attain his salvation only in society, and by the memory—though vague and secularized—of God's promises in favor of one people which He called His own.

The Church claims for itself the prerogative of being this people of God en route to its destiny—the heavenly city. "God's people en route" would be approved by Paul as a fitting description of the Church: *people,* that is, a society; the people *of God* —summoned and brought together by God and hence in nowise comparable with any merely natural society; *en route*—it has left its earthly point of departure and has not yet reached its heavenly haven of rest. In these two phrases, "no longer" and "not yet," is contained the whole drama which is proper to the Pauline concept of Christianity and, indeed, to every real concept of Christianity.

In order to approach Paul's thought even more closely, it is well to devise a second "definition": the Church is the earthly body of the heavenly Christ, her Head, filled with His Spirit and laden with His powers.

110

Let us now try to explain and justify as briefly as possible both these descriptions of the Pauline idea of the Church.

I. *Juridical Versus Spiritual Church*

There are certain factors which make it easier for us—Catholics of our day—than for earlier generations to penetrate into the ideas of the Apostle concerning Christ's Church. We are children of our age and its spirit. For the past half century, even within the Church itself there have been tendencies which have awakened the true Christian consciousness of solidarity. Such are the Eucharistic and liturgical movements, which have again drawn our attention to the inner life of the Church as a supernatural society. Such are the powerful missionary endeavors, which clearly outline for all the faithful the universality, the extent, and the organization of the Church. Such is the Catholic Action movement, which has reminded us of the apostolic duty and responsibility of the laity. All these are not new. Indeed, they are as old as the Church. But in recent times they have been revitalized in new forms and with new consciousness, as though they had just been discovered. Let us give another proof of how the creative and vivifying Spirit of God remains active in old Mother Church, which, though injured and torn through the human

111

(much too human!) element of almost twenty centuries, has always found within itself—that is, in Christ—the strength of rejuvenation which makes her ever young. The encyclical of Pius XII on the mystical body of Christ has set an official seal on this new life and salutary consciousness and has expressed it in clear formulas. Appearing in the summer of 1943, amidst the nerve-racking episodes of the Second World War, it reminded us that the world with all its turmoil and its misery will pass away and that the Church will overcome all the attacks of the powers of hell.

Paul's ideas on the Church do not, however, fully coincide with ours. To a certain extent this is inevitable. One cannot easily dismiss a difference of so many centuries, whose course has witnessed the development of a complete theological system. But there is yet another reason. The notion which the majority of Catholics have of the Church is still too external and too superficial, in spite of all the favorable elements of the past period. We are always too much inclined to think of the Church as an organization, an institution, or, what is worse, an agency of power. Furthermore, we consider her as something static. In our estimation she has become too much a specific, historical power, rooted in this world side by side with others. We look upon her as fixed to the earth. We are not sufficiently cognizant of her spiritual character. Paul can heal us of this affliction.

Before we attempt to express in our own words the thoughts proper to the Apostle, it is well to clarify one point beforehand and thus avoid all possible misunderstanding. Paul does not recognize a Church which is *purely spiritual*. He does not conceive of a society without authority and organization. There has been a tendency among certain Protestant circles, which have had some influence upon Catholics, especially German Catholics, to create opposition between a *juridical* Church and a *spiritual* Church. They say that what Jesus intended, and what Paul had in mind, was not a firmly organized society that was to defy the ages, but a purely religious movement; and that it was never their intention to give a definite form to the indefinite groups of their followers, but rather some sort of temporary unity for the short period which was to intervene till the second coming of the Lord. In his communities of Christians, Paul would not recognize an established authority properly so-called but rather *charismatici,* persons who, under the influence of a certain enthusiasm or ecstasy, exercised leadership in special cases and in a peculiar manner. But these special gifts were not attached to a specific hierarchy. Paul's Christianity was truly a society of love without laws and without institutions, united through a certain inner spirit. Only in later times, as the original zeal waned and the second coming did not occur, did the Church undergo the common lot of all spiritual movements. There was an attempt to stabilize this free movement of the Spirit under fixed forms and to regulate it with certain norms. The spontaneous impulses of love were supplanted by a human code of morals; faith was rationalized through theological formulas, and laws were substituted for Christian freedom. In this process—the result of which was the Catholic Church with its powerful and detailed hierarchy and organization—Rome played the leading role. The capital of the Old World empire became the center of Western Christianity (the Romans always have had a peculiar genius for law and special gifts for organization and rule). The primacy of the Bishop of Rome is, in the last analysis, no more than the result of an inevitable historical evolution which can easily be traced. The Latin Church became the most active part of Christianity and set its seal upon that Western Catholicism which dominates the Church.

One cannot deny that there are certain elements of truth in this theory. Without doubt the Church is *also* a human society and therefore subject, to a certain extent, to the laws which rule all human institutions. Whenever such institutions expand in time and place, the first enthusiasm wanes and is frequently followed by a sort of paralysis. Who would dare say that the spirit of Francis of Assisi has been preserved absolutely, without blemish, in the many and different groups that bear his name? Moreover, what right thinking man would dare say that that was at all *possible?* The marvel of the Church consists precisely in this: that, in spite of being composed of weak men, she nevertheless always succeeds in revitalizing herself to such an extent that one is reminded of her original luster. A John Bosco, a Curé D'Ars, to mention but a few, may vie with even the greatest charismatics of Paul's time and will perhaps surpass them by the pure, spiritual character of their sanctity.

It is likewise foolish to deny that the Church of today is endlessly more complicated and more minutely organized than in the early days or that she now presents an entirely different appearance. She is a *living* organization and, as Newman says, change is a basic law of all life. We may even add that life means change with the retention only of the kernel. It is absolutely *impossible* that the Christianity of Paul's day should have manifested the externals of the Catholic Church today: the organization of the Church was still in its very first stage and comparatively quite simple; it embraced a small minority of people who spoke one language, knew only one civilization, and were citizens of the same empire. Whoever asks himself whether he can recognize the structure of our universal Church in Paul's little communities, really puts the question wrongly. He ought rather to ask: Is it possible to detect the *beginnings* of hierarchic orders and juridical organization in Paul's epistles? Can we demonstrate that in his time the nucleus of all this was already present, at least in the bud? Were not even this possible, we need not be unduly alarmed; for we must remember that the epistles are only letters of occasion, of which some have been lost and others preserved. At the most, they give us only an incomplete picture of the life of the Church in those days. However, it is not impossible to detect these *beginnings*. The so-called Pastoral Epistles, those to Timothy and Titus written shortly before Paul's death, are full of detailed instructions concerning the organization of the churches. Timothy and Titus were his dearest disciples, bishops respectively of Ephesus and Crete, as tradition tells us. They were given all sorts of admonitions regarding the purity of doctrine and the choice of priests, deacons, and other ecclesiastical personages. The rational critics deny the Pauline origin of these epistles. One must admit that their tone is entirely different from, say, the Epistle to the Romans. But is that a reason for surprise? The Apostle sees himself standing at death's door. He is desirous of consolidating his life's work. He does not write directly to the churches concerning the great problems of faith and justification, but rather to two trusted disciples who know his mind but who, at the same time, need concrete and practical instruction for what more and more resembles the ordinary care of souls. It is now no longer a question of conquering, but *rather* of keeping and fortifying one's position. The second generation of Christianity is now at hand.

Even his earlier epistles show evident traces of a hierarchic beginning and an ever-growing organization of ecclesiastical life. The churches which were founded by Paul remained subject to his apostolic authority from the very beginning. His authority solved all questions as a last instance. This is so even in the church which is preferably cited as the model of a free, charismatic society—that of the troublesome brothers and sisters of Corinth. In none of his earlier epistles does Paul manifest his authority more firmly than in those to the Corinthians. He prescribes regulations for the celebration of the Eucharist, for the ordering of the charismatic gifts,

117

for collections, and even for the dress of women. He excommunicates public sinners. He appeals to the customs of other churches as a standard for the Corinthians. Likewise before the Pastoral Epistles, he acknowledges superiors in the local churches. This is expressly stated in the inscription of the Epistle to the Philippians.

Nonetheless it is true that, in his idea of the Church, these elements occupy a subordinate place, and that his attention is drawn by the very nature of the matter to other, more essential, aspects. For this reason it is of prime importance that we fully understand his ideas on the Church and, as it were, make them our own. This will be our next task.

II. *God's People en Route*

Of all New Testament writers, Paul uses the word *church, ecclesia,* the most. Generally it means local churches, "communities"; occasionally, however, especially in the Captivity Epistles, it means the Church as a whole, the universal Church. This last notion is fundamental. The Church is not the sum of local communities. These, rather, represent the Church on a small scale, as is apparent, for example, from the imagery of a betrothal that is applied to a particular community (II Cor. 11:2). Etymologically, the word *ecclesia* does not possess

that static nuance which we often attribute to it.[1]
For the Greeks it originally signified a democratic
gathering of the people, not the community as such,
but rather a gathering of free citizens summoned
together by heralds. It had no religious significance
whatever. The Christian usage is not derived hence,
but has its origin in the Greek Bible, the translation
of the Old Testament, the so-called Septuagint,
which exercised an inestimable influence on ancient
Christianity. With the words *ecclesia Kuriou,* "the
church or community of God," the Septuagint rendered the Hebrew expression which was indicative
of the old Israelitic people in their special aspect of
community of cult—a gathering, in the sanctuary,
of Jahve's people, called by Him and gathered for
Him. Here we detect certain elements which later
were transferred into Paul's concept of the Church.
The ecclesia is a gathering; it is holy, it is summoned
together by God. This last element is the most important—so important that, even in Old Testament
Jewry, many were constantly and clearly aware that
this vocation was not absolutely synonymous with
corporal descent. The foremost members of the Jewish race, such as the prophets and some circles of
pious people which have left us the apocryphal writ-

[1] In the original Greek, the word *ecclesia,* church, signified a
gathering which met at a certain time and in a certain place,
rather than a permanent and established community.

ings, understood that the larger mass of Jews would not be saved, in spite of the fact that originally the people as a whole had been chosen by God. The majority of the chosen people did not live according to God's law and good pleasure, and would not be able to withstand the wrath of the day of Jahve, the judgment of God, which would introduce the Messianic period. Only a *remnant* would be saved and share the blessings of this last age. These pious people looked upon themselves as the *remnant,* as God's people properly speaking, as the minority which remained faithful to Him, thanks to His calling. God's choice was the basis of their election from the masses and of their sanctity. They even called themselves *the saints,* not indeed with pharisaical overestimation, but in virtue of their consciousness of the divine calling. Thus the prophet Daniel, in the well-known vision of the four beasts and the son of man, saw "one like the son of man coming on the clouds of heaven" (Dan. 7:13), unharmed, in spite of the fury of the monsters of the abyss, to receive domination and glory from the Ancient of days. This image of the son of man signifies, as the prophet himself declared (7:21), "the saints," the community of the last period.

This consciousness of being God's saints, His chosen ones, His "Church" and society, existed from the first in the ancient church at Jerusalem, as we are told in the first chapters of the Acts of the Apostles. This ancient church regarded itself as the ideal Israel in God's design, as the only rightful successor of the Synagogue. The first Christians called themselves the saints, the Church of God. The final age had begun. The Spirit had been given abundantly to the small group of apostles and disciples and remained active among them. In them had been fulfilled the great promises of the Spirit, of which almost all the prophets had spoken, and which were to be the sign of the great transformation. In the midst of an evil and distorted generation they constituted the chosen group; they were His beloved, His saints, who had received the Spirit as pledge and were expecting a glorious accomplishment of all things through Jesus' second coming.

This is the origin of Paul's idea of the Church. He uses the same terminology: *ecclesia* of God— that is, a society and gathering called together by God. He also speaks of the Christians, especially those of Jerusalem, as saints, the elect and beloved of God (Rom. 1:7; 15:26; I Cor. 1:2; 16:1; Col. 3:12, etc.). For him likewise, the foundation of Christianity is the divine calling, which has already segregated them from the present age. In his mind, the Church is the society of the last age, one no longer rooted in the present world order but already filled with the power of a new era and living in hope, since completion has not yet come. There is only this difference, that, in accordance with his special vocation and life's work, he especially emphasizes the fact that the pagans who believe will also constitute a part of this people of God, together with the remnant of Israel that was saved (Rom. 11:5, 17–24). For Paul, one of the wonders of the divine mysteries is the fact that "the Gentiles are joint heirs, and fellow-members of the same body, and joint partakers of the promise in Christ Jesus through the gospel" (Eph. 3:6). "For in Christ Jesus neither circumcision nor uncircumcision but a new creation is of any account" (Gal. 6:15).

Of special importance to us Catholics of the twentieth century are two facts which give particular meaning to this primitive but vivid concept. The first is that essentially the Church is constituted, or called together, by virtue of divine election. In our age and surroundings, now that the circumstances in which the Church is living are so different from those of Paul's age, it would seem that membership in the Church is largely a matter of birth and background. Undoubtedly these factors do play an important part in a society that is basically Christian. Yet even for us it is true that God's *calling* constitutes us His beloved and His saints, and unites us in God's society, His Church. This is true even though at present the plan of God's grace generally flows through the normal and quiet channels of birth from Catholic parents, of Catholic background and schooling. The Church is not a natural classification, but a special creation of God; and we are well aware that even the man who has been reared a Catholic will be faced, at least once if not several times, with the deliberate choice of obedience to the faith.

The second fact may be called the eschatological element. Now that the Church has existed for nineteen centuries, even the majority of Christians believe that the end of the world will come through the atom bomb rather than through the second coming of our Lord. Who will say what means the Lord will employ as He opens the curtain on the last scene? But, as St. Peter says, a thousand years are as one day in the sight of God. The determining factor is not whether the end will come tomorrow or after a hundred years, but that the end will come, an end which for us will mean accomplishment, the beautiful completion of all things. The Church has been instituted in view of this end. Her inner power drives her toward this accomplishment. She is, by the very nature of her constitution, God's people en route. In spite of everything, especially of the human

123

element within her, she has cut loose her earthly moorings and is on the way to her heavenly port. That is her state of being, and likewise ours. We are travelers, *viatores;* and, though a bit more mud than is absolutely necessary may stick to our feet, we are on the way and our eyes must be directed toward that distant land, while our hands are busied close by. "And the spirit and the bride say, 'Come!' And let him who hears say 'Come!' " (Apoc. 22:17). "Maranatha, come, Lord Jesus!" (I Cor. 16:22). "May Your grace come and the world pass" (*Didache*).

III. *The Mystical Body*

We are all aware that the doctrine presenting the Church as the mystical body of Christ finds its strongest basis in the epistles of Paul. The encyclical of Pius XII has confirmed the opinion of theologians that, in this teaching, we may study the most intimate nature of the Church. What we perhaps do not know is how the Apostle arrived at these formulas and how he himself only gradually attained a wider and deeper insight into this mystery. It began as simple and ordinary imagery. He never used the expression *mystical body.* This came only later with a desire to distinguish clearly between the mystical body of Christ, His Church, and His real body in the Eucharist.

Paul compares the Church with the human body for the first time in the Epistle to the Romans and in the First Epistle to the Corinthians which was written shortly afterwards. The occasion was again the question of the charisms. These special gifts of the Holy Ghost occupied an important and striking place in the ecclesiastical life of that day. They differed greatly in their manifestation and operation, including, as they did, the power of miracles, prophecy, the gift of tongues, extraordinary knowledge in matters of faith, and other gifts. Yet, says Paul, in their origin and destination they are but one. They all come from God and serve for the good of the community, for the benefit of the Church. They are not spiritual favors bestowed for the personal honor and glory of their fortunate possessors, but they must serve the whole community; otherwise they are superfluous and even harmful, an occasion for aversion, ambition, and division. Moreover, charity surpasses them all. These particular gifts of the Spirit manifest the diversity and the wealth of God's works in the Church, but they must all contribute to that one great end: the welfare of the community. To illustrate this point, he uses the image of the body. "For just as in one body we have many members, yet all the members have not the same function, so we, the many, are one body in Christ, but severally members one of another" (Rom. 12:4–8). And to the Corinthians he wrote exactly the same (I Cor. 12:12–31). This is really quite ordinary; there is nothing special about it—particularly if we remember that such imagery was common in antiquity and was used in connection with the commonweal of the Roman Empire. Paul merely adapts it to the particular society with which he is dealing. To this society he also adapts the fable of the contention between the subordinate members, which was equally common in stoic propaganda. To the Corinthians he writes: "Now if they were all one member, where would the body be? But as it is, there are indeed many members, yet but one body. And the eye cannot say to the hand, 'I do not need thy help'; nor again the head to the feet, 'I have no need of you.' Nay, much rather, those that seem the more feeble members of the body are more necessary; and those that we think the less honorable members of the body we surround with more abundant honor, and our uncomely parts receive a more abundant comeliness, whereas our comely parts have no need of it. But God has so tempered the body together in due portion as to give more abundant honor where it was lacking; that there may be no disunion in the body, but that the members may have care for one another" (I Cor. 12:19–25).

Thus the comparison is commonplace, and Paul is comparing to a body only the faithful of a local church. And yet, even here we detect other elements which will burst the shell of the commonly used image; even here this common image is elevated and absorbed by Paul's leading ideas on the mystery of Christ and on the redemption. The image of a body, with which he permits the churches of Rome and Corinth to coincide (for that is what he does at the end), is more than a mere point of comparison. The Spirit causes the unity of the body. Not only does the Spirit unite the believer individually with Christ in baptism (I Cor. 6:11; Rom. 6:1), but He also unites the believers with each other in one Christian unity. "For in one Spirit we were all baptized into one body, whether Jews or Gentiles, whether slaves or free; and we were all given to drink of one Spirit" (I Cor. 12:13). With equal right he asserts that Christ constitutes the unity of that body, "for the Lord is the Spirit" (II Cor. 3:17). This body, he tells us, is "of Christ" (I Cor. 12:27), or "in Christ" (Rom. 12:5). It may even be called simply "Christ" (I Cor. 12:12). This is what he tells us, without any further ado and without any special preparation, in a remarkable little sentence that comes almost as an

127

afterthought: "For as the body is one and has many members, and all the members of the body, many as they are, form one body, *so also it is with Christ.*" Yet this is always something different from what Seneca writes to Nero: "You are the soul (animus) of your community, which is your body." The body which Paul has in mind is not a natural body or some unity effected by human effort, but a spiritual (pneumatic) unity, which has its central point in Christ and is identified with Him in some manner. Even the first time the Apostle uses this image, it spontaneously touches upon the great truths of Christ and the Spirit and attains a new significance. The vagueness of the expression is the best proof that the relationships between the Head, Christ, and the body, the Church, are not yet consciously seen. On the other hand, whenever it comes in contact with this general image, Christian reflection on the different aspects of that body flows almost automatically from Paul's teaching.

This Pauline doctrine actually follows in two of the Captivity Epistles, that to the Colossians and that to the Ephesians. Perhaps we must thank a Jewish-Gnostic error, which had begun to find acceptance among the Christians of Colossa, an unimportant city of Asia Minor, for Paul's most beautiful teaching on the Church. As one might expect from

128

a man of Paul's caliber, it was a reaction which far surpassed the occasion in importance. It seems that these people held the opinion that redemption through Christ was not sufficient. The Judaizers of the Epistle to the Galatians had a similar opinion; in their mind the Law and circumcision had to be added. Among the Colossians there was some difference. They were of the opinion that Christ did excellent work in His sphere, but that He Himself was nonetheless not in a position to unite man to God. Since God Himself is absolutely unapproachable, to effect a union it was necessary to honor and reconcile many spiritual powers, perhaps we should say angels, which occupied an intermediate position between God and man. These angels were a sort of emanation, a radiation of the great Unknown, and they bridged the chasm between God and the world. Together they formed the pleroma, the fulness, the totality of divine powers which were to save man. Christ was only one of many. In any case, He was not above them; and by Himself He could not be the pleroma.

It was this concept—strange, perhaps, to the modern man, but deeply rooted in the religious sentiment of that time—which Paul combatted in his Epistle to the Colossians. Shortly after, he reviewed, as it were, the whole complexity of themes, this time in a calmer manner and without the excitement of controversy. Then he set down the result of his meditations as a profound synthesis, a grand hymn on the Church, in his Epistle to the Ephesians. Let us try to outline briefly the leading thoughts of the Apostle, though this can hardly be done with full justice. It were much better to read, to study, and to contemplate these epistles in their entirety.

He leaves no room for doubt that Christ is not only above all men, but also above all spiritual powers. "[God hath raised Christ] from the dead, and set him at his right hand in heaven above every Principality and Power and Virtue and Domination —in short, above every name that is named, not only in this world, but also in that which is to come. And all things he made subject under his feet" (Eph. 1:20–22). In Christ, he says, dwells all the fulness of the divinity, bodily.[2] There really is no question of angels at all. "He is the image of the invisible God, the firstborn of every creature. For in him were created all things in the heavens and on the earth, things visible and things invisible, whether Thrones, or Dominations, or Principalities, or Powers. All things have been created through and unto him, and

[2] This last phrase is a stab at the false spirituality of the heretics. According to some, the word *somatikos* here signifies *true, real.*

130

he is before all creatures, and in him all things hold together" (Col. 1:15–17). This seems sufficiently clear.

To this Paul adds: "Again, he is the head of his body, the Church" (Col. 1:18; Eph. 1:22–23). This means that absolute sovereignty over the Church belongs to the heavenly Lord, to the glorified Kyrios. It also means much more. He is also her Redeemer, who delivered Himself unto death for her sake to win Himself an immaculate bride (Eph. 5:23–27). He is the source of her growth and her life, "from which" (Eph. 4:16; Col. 2:19) and "unto which" (Eph. 4:15) the "increase and building up" of His body is accomplished through His Spirit (Eph. 2: 22; 4:4) and through love (Eph. 4:16). Thus He is not only Lord and Master of the Church, but also the very source of her life. Here we find ourselves far from the customary image of the body: we are dealing primarily with the relation of the head with the body which was seldom mentioned in the earlier letters. The erroneous teaching at Colossa had compelled Paul to reflect on this point. On the one hand, he emphasizes the truth he taught at an earlier period: that the man Christ is glorified by God and exalted on His right hand in heaven, for, even as man, Jesus is far superior to the angels. On the other, Paul is in no way desirous of bypassing

131

Christ's internal penetration of the ecclesiastical community (through His Spirit). In his Epistle to the Ephesians he develops this particular idea more than ever before and thus he adheres with almost inexpressible anxiety to the two aspects of the supernatural reality which appear almost to exclude each other. Christ is infinitely exalted by God above all things, above all thought. He is the heavenly Head of the Church doing battle here on earth. But at the same time, He is most intimately united with her as the one from whom she draws her life, as the one who completely fills and dominates her with His heavenly power. The Church, Paul says, "is his body, the fulness of him who is wholly fulfilled in all" (Eph. 1:23). She is His pleroma, as He is the pleroma of God. She is, as it were, magnetized by His power. In her the believer detects the fulness of Christ—which is to say, the fulness of heavenly life and union with God.

She is also His bride, Paul says, and "even thus ought husbands to love their wives as their own bodies. He who loves his own wife, loves himself. For no one ever hated his own flesh; on the contrary he nourishes his body, made from his flesh and from his bones" (Eph. 5:28–30). Thus, according to Paul, this image does not only signify that there is a sort of idealized state of love between

Christ and the Church. He views it much more realistically. The Church is, as it were, the very flesh of Christ, one with Him and necessarily nourished and cherished by Him.

To put it in one word: the Church here on earth is Christ's all. In the eyes of the Apostle she is, as it were, the continuous incarnation of her heavenly Master.[3] In his eyes she is, as a modern spiritual writer has expressed it, "The all and the very sphere of life of every believer." [4]

As long as we are here on earth we must strive for a better society. In this effort we have the example and leadership of all the popes of recent times. The Catholic must make his contribution wholeheartedly. The Church will not fail in this task, even though it may seem that her voice exercises scarcely any influence in the world today—if, indeed, it was fully heeded at any time. But Paul teaches us that this age

[3] It is difficult to avoid all misunderstanding when one tries to give expression to the highest and noblest truths of our religion. That is why we say that the Church is, *as it were,* the continuous incarnation of her Master. Strictly speaking, there is only one incarnation, that of the Divine Word in the pure womb of the Immaculate Virgin. Strictly speaking, Christ is not identical with the Church. On the other hand, the union of Christ with His Church is so intimate that it permits one to speak as above, thus following the example of the Apostle himself, who called the Church the body of Christ and His fulness. See L. Cerfaux, *La théologie de l'Eglise,* page 264.

[4] H. Clerissac, *Le mystère de l'Eglise,* Paris, 1925, p. 3.

is evil and will remain evil as long as, and insofar as, Christ does not rule. He also teaches that Christ, though ascended into heaven, rules here on earth and effects salvation and gives life through His body, the Church, which is filled with His Spirit. Whether the world will accept the salutary influence of the Church remains God's secret. Outside the Church, viewed not merely as an organization, but above all, and especially, as a society of love and as the fulness of Christ, endowed with earthly existence, there is no thinkable salvation for man. This is the mystery, Paul says, which God had purposed for the fulness of time: "To re-establish all things in Christ, both those in the heavens and those on earth" (Eph. 1: 9–10).

Index of Scripture Texts *

* Bold face page numbers indicate that the text is quoted more or less in full on those pages.

135

INDEX

INDEX

INDEX

A NOTE ON THE TYPE

IN WHICH THIS BOOK WAS SET

This book is set in Intertype Garamond, a type face considered by many as one of the most successful ever introduced. Claude Garamond, the designer of these beautiful types, was a pupil of Geofroy Tory, a leader of the Renaissance in France, a university professor, artist, designer and printer who set out to place French on an equal footing with Latin and Greek as a language of culture. Garamond's evenness of color throughout the font is highly appreciated by book designers. The moderately strong fine lines tend to soften the effect, which is decidedly agreeable to many. One thing is certain, Garamond is unusually pleasing and will distinguish much good printing for many years to come. This book was composed by the York Composition Company, Inc., of York, Pa., and bound by Moore and Company of Baltimore. The typography and design of this book are by Howard N. King.